D0948105

CULTURAL INTELLIGENCE IN THE 21ST CENTURY

DRIVING INCLUSION, REVENUE, AND ESG

STEPHAN M. BRANCH, MBA, CEO

Post Hill
PRESS

A POST HILL PRESS BOOK
ISBN: 978-1-63758-974-8
ISBN (eBook): 978-1-63758-975-5

Cover design by Conroy Accord

Post Hill Press
New York • Nashville
posthillpress.com

Published in the United States of America
1 2 3 4 5 6 7 8 9 10

This book is dedicated to four people who have had the most significant impact on me personally and on my career.

My mother, Bobbye Brewer Branch, taught me what unconditional love is and that people should not ever think of others as more or less than themselves, regardless of ethnicity, color, or socioeconomic status. She taught me to see value in every person, and she gave me my curiosity about other cultures and my thirst for knowledge. I've spent much of my life trying to figure out how she did it. I believe this book tells that story. RIP Mother.

Because of my Gen Z son Sebastian, I strive to be the best version of myself in all ways, always. I am grateful for the countless conversations we've had and for the ones we will have because you make me a more empathetic and enlightened person. I am proud of you for always being true to yourself, and I love you unconditionally and for infinity.

To Mon Ami, thank you for joining me on this journey. You have been there the entire way and have always given me the support I needed to be the global nomad I was born to be. I wouldn't have taken nearly as many risks nor had nearly as many amazing adventures without you, and your presence on this journey is what made this book possible. Thank you for being you.

Glenda Ballard, my mentor and my son's Godmother, who taught me as a naïve college freshman that I could write, that I was capable, and could add value through my writing. She gave me confidence in myself as a student, and she gave me my love for writing. I wouldn't be where I am today without having had her as *that* teacher who changed my life forever.

Table of Contents

Special Acknowledgment

THERE IS BUT ONE PERSON that deserves to stand alone on this page because I wouldn't have done it without him—Chris Richardson.

You made this book eminently more substantive and provocative than it otherwise might have been. You were somehow able to take all of my personal experiences and stories, your own research, and curriculum from our digital solutions along with shared stories from amazing CEOs and global leaders from around the world, and weave it all together into something profoundly gripping.

Chris and I have been good friends and colleagues for decades, and he is also my son's Godfather. He was the right choice to co-write this book with me because he is a prolific writer, and he has the three most important ingredients needed in a person to become a successful global leader: empathy, a global mindset, and a thirst for knowledge. You'll soon find out what a brilliant storyteller he is as well. Now residing in Athens, Greece, Chris is a true global nomad who has amassed extraordinary personal stories (some of which are shared in this book while others were too spicy to include) from his time living in places such as Paris, Geneva, Zurich, New York, Sydney, London, Toronto, and Kassel, Germany. *Gracias por todo mi Cuñado*.

Introduction

IF YOU ARE A CEO or a manager, or you work on a team in a global organization, raising your cultural intelligence by learning nine cultural competencies will transform every part of your business, including how you develop strategy; how you lead; how you win business; how you interact with your customers; how you build your brand; how you market; and, yes, how you build cultures of inclusion on a global scale while simultaneously increasing your ESG (environmental, social, and governance) rating, revenue, and overall company valuation. The *S* in ESG isn't only about social equity. It's also about understanding the importance of how business gets done in other countries. Did you know you can resolve both while having a transformative financial impact on your organization? How can you build a globally inclusive culture in an organization where everyone feels seen, heard, and respected if you don't even understand how cultures communicate differently, build relationships differently, and cultivate trust and respect differently?

In recent years, organizations have become fixated on ESG because they recognize that the millennial generation is largely focused on investing in companies that have higher ESG ratings, as those organizations better align with their philosophies, and their desire to do good things with their money. No doubt the Z and Alpha generations feel the same way. Global 2000 companies know this and are redirecting much of their focus to the *S* in ESG in order to drive up their ESG ratings. Historically, it has been much more challenging to demonstrate improvement in the *S* because of a lack of metrics that show an increase in a quantifiable and verifiable way.

Who cares, you may ask?

Well, higher ESG ratings typically mean higher share prices and higher company valuation. Global 2000 companies know this, which is why there has been such an intense focus on this recently. That's also why European and Asian companies are now becoming more focused on creating cultures of belonging and inclusion necessary to drive up their ESG ratings. They now recognize that this conversation is much more important than they thought, and they see how it's impacting the company's share price. They no longer see this as just a "US discussion."

I've lived on five continents and worked in well over fifty countries with full P&L responsibilities in both privately held and publicly traded multibillion-dollar companies. I've taken companies public while simultaneously creating the explosive growth required to meet the very high expectations of investors and boards. Jack Welch (retired chairman and CEO of General Electric) sat on the board of one of those companies early in my career, so I know from firsthand experience the pressure to deliver results. Throughout my career, people have wondered how I could deliver those results so quickly. They have often said I made it look so easy. The secret has and always will be that I fully grasp how leadership, cultural intelligence, and inclusion coalesce to create extraordinary leaders with the capacity to make a transformative impact on the business and the bottom line.

When I coach business leaders on the Fortune 1000, they often tell me that their HR leaders are clueless because they don't fully understand the day-to-day business challenges involved in leading global teams and working in other countries. I often find that the three most critical challenges global leaders identify as they lead while trying to simultaneously create inclusive cultures and build significant revenue growth are the following: *working across cultures in different parts of the world; establishing team effectiveness and cohesion, especially for global teams;* and *understanding business norms in other cultures and how those norms play out in the business units.* However, ask almost any HR leader, and they will say that their leadership program is so well developed that they don't need to understand how business is done differently in other cultures. Another one that always brings a smile to my face is when they say, "We do things our way," or "We do things the [XYZ] company way," or "We do things the [Dutch, German, Japanese, etc.] way." To those organizations, I'd suggest you may have chosen the wrong people to sit in those global HR roles. They are missing a crucial part of the equation if they don't understand how country culture impacts an entire organization, including *global* leadership, team effectiveness, and team cohesion.

This is alarming because talent, L&D, and diversity officers function as internal consultants supporting the business units, and these leaders are short on time. They need just-in-time learning to solve specific business problems. Without the support of an HR team that fully understands the impact cultural differences have on the business, leaders are left to their own devices to figure it out. So, that is precisely what we will do together in this book.

Chapter 1

GLOBALIZATION MADE CULTURAL ASSUMPTIONS OF THE 20TH CENTURY OBSOLETE

Many members of today's business world still rely on cultural norms and social conclusions that were drawn in the second half of the 20th century. During this period, most companies were just beginning to globalize their activities and staffing. This was a time that preceded the widespread use of the internet, social media, and any kind of conversation about cultural differences or inclusion in the workplace. The criteria used in the late 20th century for looking at culture assumed that every individual from a given country acted, believed, and worked similarly. Yet, in today's business world, we do business more and more in other countries. Today's hyperconnectivity defies any map and any politician's proclamation. The trend was accelerated as a result of the COVID-19 pandemic. This has caused companies to create organizational structures of remote workers in multiple locations that would have previously been thought too diverse for team cohesion.

In the 21st century, we are living in a place where someone sitting late at night in their living room in Athens can watch the news at sunrise in Sydney live online. We live in a time of digital nomads able to legally work in far-flung countries that are completely dissimilar from their own. We live in a time of increased awareness of those who may be disadvantaged based on their identity and circumstances. This includes everything from striving to achieve an appropriate gender balance at the board level to recognizing the employees of an enterprise who may be confined to a wheelchair or a member of the LGBTQ+ community.

In short, we live on a planet where fewer people fit into routine cultural and social categories. The future belongs to companies that take an inclusive approach to their economic governance, the environment, and the social aspects of everything they do. As stated above, these criteria are commonly abbreviated as ESG when defined as the key factors enabling a business to thrive. Companies are ultimately a reflection of the people that work within them. The key frontline stakeholders of any business are its employees. Therefore, the benefits and rewards of paying attention to the cultural and social structure of the enterprise—the *S* of the ESG equation—can significantly outweigh the effort involved in the journey to genuine inclusion. Direct benefits include the enhanced dedication and productivity of the employees, who truly feel part of the organization. Rewards include an improved ESG rating, which can raise the share price of the company because it attracts more investors. A high-profile example is that of the coffeehouse chain Starbucks, which maintains a hiring policy that is as broad and inclusive as possible worldwide. In the United States, the company introduced a policy aimed at the recruitment of veterans. In Europe, Starbucks extends a hand to displaced individuals who are far from their home countries.

The attention to the *S* of the equation is a significant contributor to the company's success. The global profits of Starbucks have increased by 30.4 percent on average since 2020.

The practice of treating employees inclusively was observed by Howard Schultz—the interim CEO of Starbucks—as being something that "should not be viewed as an added cost that cuts into profits, but as a powerful energizer that can grow the enterprise into something far greater than one leader could envision."

Enhanced cultural and social awareness leads to direct business success. As Mr. Schultz states, it is ultimately a *catalyst* for profit growth rather than a drain on the enterprise. It vastly improves the effectiveness of the leadership team, which in turn maximizes the performance of employees. This produces a stronger brand image for the company and generates increased sales and, thus, revenue. A positive side effect is improved negotiations with global suppliers, which brings a decrease in operational costs.

Today's business innovators are, therefore, those who are able—and empowered—to recognize the cultural differences in those they lead, no matter where their colleagues may be geographically or how big their teams may be. Successful business leaders in the 21st century are those who can use their cultural and social competency to embrace a holistic approach throughout the enterprise. The results and benefits of this soon become apparent.

Chapter 2

CULTURE AND COMMERCE IN THE 21ST CENTURY

GLOBALIZATION CAN BE DEFINED AS the process by which businesses and organizations operate on an international scale. Due to the increased accessibility of commercial air travel and shipping containers in the second half of the 20th century, major companies were able to adopt a worldwide corporate strategy that increased the pace and range of globalization to a degree unimaginable by corporate leaders even fifty years before. As such, international companies were required to become aware of the cultural differences of the countries in which they operated. Naturally, those companies needed a framework by which they could begin to understand the cultural dimensions. This understanding of the dimensions was derived from studies among corporate employees. The countries of the world were each characterized by standard actions and values. While not factually incorrect, these conclusions can nevertheless be classified as stereotypes.

The corporate leaders of the day understood that countries with similar historical backgrounds and a common language tend to possess cultural similarities. They understood that countries with a shared border tend to be more akin in cultural terms than those that are far apart geographically. Added to this basic premise were standard cultural observations about such dimensions as hierarchy and timekeeping. These cultural norms were assumed to apply to every member of society in a given country. These conclusions offered a partial insight into cultural and social issues that were useful to the corporate leaders of the late 20th century.

Then came the 21st century and the widespread use of the internet in every corner of the world. This would cause globalization to exponentially accelerate in a way that would touch everyone. Globalization was no longer just about corporate assumptions and policy, for it had begun to reach individuals in myriad ways outside of the workplace and in their daily lives.

Yet many of the cultural and social assumptions of the business world are still essentially tied to the belief that—for instance—everyone in the United States thinks one way or that all Germans are culturally and socially identical. This is no longer viable in today's business world, for the narrative has moved on. Thanks to both large-scale international migration and local societal changes, demographic landscapes are changing in countless ways and countless locations. While some may resist this new reality of globalization, there is no going back to the 20th century. Today's hyperconnectivity across borders is too powerful—and popular—a force to be undone. The successful business leaders of the future will be those who recognize this.

LARGE-SCALE CULTURAL MIGRATIONS

There have been a number of examples of large-scale international migrations in the late 20th century and the early 21st century. It is useful to look at two of them to appreciate how the cultural assumptions involving the countries at each end of the migrant's journey are not automatically or universally applicable in such scenarios.

i) Greeks in Australia

Greek settlers first arrived in Australia in the "gold rush" days of the 1850s. However, in the 1950s and 1960s, that migration from Greece to Australia increased exponentially. A migration scheme adopted by the Australian government was designed to increase the population of the country following the Second World War. While many Greek Australians hold on to what they call "politicos mas" (our culture), what constitutes Greek tradition in the "host" country has adapted and evolved. Meanwhile, Greece itself continues to evolve in the absence of those that have left the country. Therefore, some of the closely held traditions of the diaspora may be found to be "out-of-date" in Greece they have left behind. This means that routine cultural assumptions about Australia and Greece do not accurately reflect the individuals involved at both ends of the migratory flow. This can be a critical misjudgment, given that Melbourne is today the largest Greek city outside of Greece itself. Some 10 percent of its population of five million people are of Greek origin and therefore do not readily fit into any routine categorization of Australian culture.

Case Study

> Kostas recently migrated from Athens to Sydney to become a junior doctor in one of the city hospitals. He was happy to find that—while smaller than the Greek community in Melbourne—

Sydney provided plenty of opportunities to connect with Greeks who had migrated there in the middle of the 20th century. At the same time, Kostas found that the characteristics of these elder Greek migrants most closely associated with their cultural identities—such as membership in the Greek Orthodox Church and enjoyment of traditional music—were more prominent in Sydney than they now were in the Athens of the 21st century. Kostas found that the first-generation offspring of the mid-20th-century Greek migrants were integrated into mainstream Australian culture and society. Nonetheless, the above aspects of the Greek lifestyle were still emphasized as important—even by the younger first-generation individuals—in Australia more than by young people in Greece today. This highlights the fact that cultures and societies are in a state of constant flux. For instance, since the large-scale migration of Greeks to Australia in the mid-20th century, Greece has become a fully integrated member state of the European Union (EU). This has impacted Greek cultural norms given the high level of migration within EU member states by outbound Greeks and inbound EU nationals.

ii) *Worldwide Expatriates in Dubai*

There are also more continuous international movements of persons that take place over long periods of time. One example is the steady increase of foreign nationals going to live and work in Dubai. The primary commercial hub of the United Arab Emirates (UAE), Dubai has the highest number of resident expatriates of any city in the world (measured as a percentage of its population). In 1975, 64 percent of the city's residents were foreign nationals. Today, some 85 percent of the population of Dubai was born in some other country. The largest number of resident expatriates in the city hail from Bangladesh, India, and Pakistan. Many British, French, Filipino, South African, and United States nationals call Dubai home. This kaleidoscope of cultures is definitely not reflected in standard cultural categorizations of the UAE. This therefore means that some three million people are being excluded from any common cultural assumptions of the country.

Case Study

Christine is a US American who has lived in Dubai for many years. She serves as the managing director of Santa Fe relocation. The employees of the company's Dubai office represent no less than fifteen nationalities: American, Argentinian, Belgian, British, Filipino, Hungarian, Indian, Iranian, Irish, Kazakhstani, Polish, Romanian, Russian, South African, Spanish, and Ukrainian. As is typical of business leaders in Dubai, Christine has to remain mindful—daily—of the various cultures involved in managing her staff. At the same time, Christine works consistently toward team cohesion. To do so, she makes sure that the team members are aware of each other's cultural differences. Concurrently Christine uses this mutual understanding to create a "unique" internal culture within the employee group based on common values and the goals of the enterprise.

21ST-CENTURY CULTURAL CATALYSTS

We can see that the world is no longer fitting into the cultural "boxes" that have become so comfortable for corporate leaders to assume. While the world's countries are still being conveniently categorized by assumed cultural norms that date from the 20th century, humanity is on the move. People are increasingly inhabiting parts of the world outside their country of origin. The internet enables companies to strive for team cohesion among remote workers in disparate locations. Simultaneously, the internet is globalizing the mindsets of those who may never have even lived in a foreign country. Three major phenomena can be observed that highlight the ever-quickening evolution of cultural interaction in the 21st century: the COVID-19 pandemic, the emergence of "digital nomad" visas, and the rise of the economic and political entity that is the European Union. All have served to accelerate intercultural exposure and the need for inclusive work practices to be introduced in global companies.

i) The COVID-19 Pandemic

The COVID-19 pandemic required companies worldwide to suddenly function with almost their entire office staff working via a laptop at home. Indeed, the European Union hurriedly published guidelines in twenty-four languages regarding cyber safety for remote workers. Although cultural factors were critical to team success, international managers often found them difficult to discern. Examples included:

- Unease among those suddenly working full-time in a language that is different from their mother tongue.

- Unease among those who are not comfortable with fully expressing themselves to a group that includes more-senior associates.

- Disparities between remote international team members in the perceived importance of punctuality.

- Disparities in the propensity of remote international team members to work productively on their own.

- Unease among those of more traditional cultures in fully expressing themselves to a group that includes s-enior female associates.

These factors impacted remote team members' performance and contributed to employee enthusiasm and a sense of belonging to the organization. As we have seen, the remote manager faces cultural and practical challenges in being effective with a diverse team of remote employees. All this is taking place in a business environment in which the number of employees working remotely will remain at levels that were unimaginable before the pandemic. By fully understanding the cultural background of team members, the manager can better appreciate—even from a distance—how each person is processing their local circumstances. As such, a distinct culture and motivational workspace for all team members can be created. Thus, despite all challenges, success can still be achieved when managing a remote international team.

Good global leaders took the time during the pandemic to learn about the home cultures of remote team members. Excellent leaders went so far as to consult with each remote team member in terms of their personal cultural background and life experiences. This has led the remote manager to better understand a diverse team and, therefore, to focus on what its members may have in common, whatever the culture or geography involved.

Simultaneously, it is imperative for remote managers to fully understand themselves from a cultural standpoint. Knowing one's own cultural propensity in terms of such dimensions as communication, hierarchy, and relationships has an enormous impact on the way one leads and manages a global team. It is only when we are aware of our assumptions and biases that we can understand those of a different culture. It should be noted that our cultural propensity comes not only from the country in which we are born but from all the experiences we may have had in our lives. The British national who has been living in Greece for twenty years is no longer going to have the cultural profile of a British person.

Studies show that such actions can lead to a 56 percent increase in job performance and a 50 percent reduction in turnover.[1] This means that the ability of managers to be effective across cultural, social, and geographical boundaries—as invisible in a virtual environment as they are real—is critical to business success. It is estimated that 70 percent of international companies offer their employees the ongoing opportunity to work remotely at least part of the time. Remote working across vast distances is here to stay, even as the impact of the COVID-19 pandemic becomes an ever-more-distant memory.

ii) Digital Nomad Visas

The sheer scale of the recent pandemic forced businesses to adjust their worldwide working methods and has led governments on every continent to look at their own practices and procedures. The most international aspect of routine governmental activity—the management of inbound immigration—has witnessed an unexpected development: the presence of an ever-increasing number of "digital nomads" in the global workforce.

Digital nomads are independent workers who embrace a location-independent, technology-enabled lifestyle that allows them to travel and work remotely anytime and anywhere they choose. Research shows that the United States alone has 4.8 million employed people who classify themselves as digital nomads (whether they are working remotely within the United States or not). The trends already mentioned above—coupled with the growth of online talent marketplaces and online information sites—have enabled more and more people to choose the digital nomad lifestyle. They tend to be a diverse group of no single generation, profession, or socioeconomic background. Research shows that just over half of the world's digital nomads are older than forty years of age and are split more or less evenly between full- and part-time workers.

With all these factors in mind, some of the world's governments have even taken the step of inventing a specific work visa to attract digital nomads to their country. The visa holders do not need to be employed in their territory in any way. However, by stipulating a certain income level, governments taking this path feel that the expenditure of digital nomads in the local economy makes the issuance of such visas worthwhile. They usually stipulate that the digital nomad possesses an international health insurance policy that covers the country involved to avoid any burden on local health systems. The number of countries offering this kind of work permit is growing yearly:

- Bermuda offers a "Work from Bermuda" visa, which allows remote workers to stay in the country for up to one year. Applicants must own a location-independent business and work remotely for a company based outside Bermuda, although there is no minimum income requirement.

- The Czech Republic offers a digital nomad visa called the "Zivno," which is valid for one year but can be extended. Applicants must be active in one of eighty government-approved professions in order to be deemed eligible for the visa. Applicants must provide proof of prearranged accommodation for at least one year, have a certain minimum amount in their bank account, and pay a small monthly amount in local taxes. Applicants must make an in-person appointment at their nearest Czech embassy or consulate.

- Dubai offers a digital nomad visa with an initial validity of one year, with the option to extend for a second successive year. There is a minimum salary requirement. Proof of private international health insurance for the UAE is also necessary.

- Estonia was the first country to create a one-year visa that allows foreigners to live in the country while working remotely. Applicants must work for a company based outside Estonia and provide proof of having met a minimum salary requirement for the previous six months. Applicants are required to complete an online application form and make an in-person appointment at their nearest Estonian embassy or consulate.

- Georgia offers the "Remotely from Georgia" visa. Applicants must own a location-independent business and/or work for a company based outside Georgia. Applicants must prove their financial ability to pay taxes in Georgia and meet a minimum salary requirement.

Such digital nomad visas are an entirely new phenomenon. The program would probably not have evolved to such an extent without the COVID-19 pandemic raising the profile of remote working around the world. Nations that do not currently offer such visas are closely monitoring the progress of countries with specific digital-nomad-visa programs and, in particular, the potentially positive effect they have on the local economy.

Those with a digital nomad visa will remain employees of an enterprise in their home country. Cultural awareness is just as important for them—in terms of their performance—as an employee on a "traditional" expatriate assignment to an overseas employer location. With time, the holder of a digital nomad visa may move on to a second or third destination—a true "nomad"— which will further enhance their cultural and geographic journey.

iii) The European Union

The most significant example of the evolution of cultures across borders can be seen in connection to the world's largest democratic experiment: the formation of twenty-seven nations into the European Union.

The EU made a key statement in 1974. Beyond its emphasis on commercial aspects, the union advised that equal attention would also be paid to the "nonmaterial" values of member countries. Through this promotion of European heritage, the EU assumed congruence between the culture, society, and territory of the bloc and therefore recognized its various cultures. The diversity of these cultures was hugely extended in 2004 with the adhesion of several former Soviet republics and Warsaw Pact countries.

The promotion of intercultural dialogue thus became a procedural mechanism within the European Parliament and the European Commission. This first manifested in most European citizens with the introduction of the "European Capital of Culture" program in 1985. The "Capital of Culture" is a city designated as such by the EU for one calendar year, during which it organizes a series of cultural events with a strong pan-European dimension. Due to the enlargement of the EU, two or three cities now hold the title each year. An increasing number of other EU policies are specifically designed to promote cultural exposure within member states.

Simultaneously, the right to move and reside in another EU country is a key factor in enabling cultural understanding and social awareness among citizens of member states. The free movement of workers is a fundamental right guaranteed by the

Treaty on the Functioning of the European Union (TFEU). Through the treaty, EU citizens are entitled to work in another country without needing a specific work permit. They may reside there for that purpose and stay after employment has terminated. They enjoy equal treatment with nationals in terms of access to employment, working conditions, and all other social and tax advantages.

The EU today is an economic and political union between twenty-seven member countries that together cover much of the continent. Beyond being an economic federation, it has evolved into an organization spanning coverage of the policy areas of climate, environment, justice, and migration. The EU has delivered more than half a century of harmony to what was for centuries a militarily deadly and socially intolerant region. On the commercial side, the EU is now the most-significant single exporter of manufactured goods and services on Earth and provides the biggest import market for over one hundred countries around the world. What makes this so remarkable is that an array of cultures—even within member countries—has been involved in achieving this.

The cultural divergence within the EU should not be underestimated. It is interesting to note how Europeans' everyday observations reflect cultural differences throughout the bloc.

- 89 percent of citizens within the twenty-seven member countries think that cultural exchanges should have a very important place in the EU so that citizens from different member countries can learn more from each other and feel more European.

- 88 percent of EU citizens think that cultural exchanges can play an important role in developing greater understanding and tolerance in the world, even where there are conflicts or tensions.

The number of EU citizens living and working in member states other than that of their birth has been increasing steadily, reaching some 15 million people (or 3.3 percent of the EU's population).[2] Many EU citizens have lived in more than one member state beyond their own, which is a growing trend. Therefore, the applicability of standard cultural norms becomes all the more inaccurate when considering such individuals.

These three striking examples show that the pace of cultural exposure and overlap is only going to increase in the 21st century. It is also going to multiply in terms of the locations involved. Again, the 20th-century cultural categorizations, originally made by country—by individuals assumed to be moving from their country of origin to one given destination—have become outdated.

SOCIAL TRENDS IN THE 21ST CENTURY

Just as cultural diversity is becoming ever more apparent in business life, social factors have also changed dramatically in the 21st century. Disadvantaged members of society—whose story would have been overlooked half a century ago—are now receiving the workplace recognition they deserve. Such individuals include military veterans, members of the LGBTQ community, and those living with a physical or psychological handicap.

Examples of relevant initiatives from around the world include:

- The government of Victoria, Australia, recognizes that companies with a diverse workforce—those embracing sexual orientation and gender identity—perform better in every way. Advisers, resources, and workshops are made available to help employers—whether large or small—on their inclusion journey.[3]

- Since 2013, any company in Germany with more than twenty employees has been required to fill at least 5 percent of its jobs with workers who are living with a disability. Medical and legal guidelines determine the degree of disability. Companies that do not fulfill the quota pay government fines, which are used to support relevant employment programs and to make public spaces accessible to disabled members of society.[4]

- The United States Center for Workforce Inclusion helps employers to better onboard military veterans by providing companies with enhanced cultural competencies. This ensures that management, employees, and HR professionals alike recognize how military culture emphasizes accountability, skill building, and teamwork.[5]

LOOKING FORWARD

It is evident that cultural dimensions by country can no longer be routinely or universally applied, whether it be in cases of large-scale migration or in individual scenarios. The accepted "categorization" of cultures—while once functional—is proving to be less and less applicable in today's business world. A fixed and unchanging view of culture that does not respond to the influences or changes of other cultures is insufficient for today's business leaders. Culture is evolving and is influenced by a variety of social and political factors that range from using social media to directing governmental actions in the countries and regions of the world.

The use of cultural norms merely leads to perpetuated stereotypes and the belief that—for instance—all US Americans think in one way and all Chinese think in another. This leads to conscious and unconscious bias. This in turn can manifest itself as indirect and unintentional discrimination toward members of a given society that belong to a group within it. This type of behavior is known as "microaggression." Due to its subtle nature, it is a very damaging form of discrimination. It is one of the key reasons why organizations strive for inclusion.

The world's countries have not maintained completely static societies—in terms of both cultural and social norms—since the nation-by-nation conclusions of the 20th century were first drawn. Countless stories of individuals—from all around planet Earth—highlight the points made above. Throughout this book, we will explore individual profiles and stories and provide examples of corporate reform and rectitude in terms of cultural and social inclusion.

Chapter 3

INCLUSION AND ITS IMPACT ON BUSINESS SUCCESS

UNDERSTANDING INCLUSION

We have observed how the cultural norms routinely adopted by companies in the 20th century are becoming less and less relevant. Therefore, it is appropriate to look at how business leaders can perform in a way that fits today's environment.

The overarching goal is to adopt a framework in business that takes a holistic view of an organization—one that seizes the opportunities of the enterprise related to environmental, social, and governance criteria. ESG is the 21st-century enhancement and integration of such corporate phenomena.

The three "pillars" of the ESG acronym can be broadly defined:

i. Environmental criteria pertain to the resilience of an enterprise in terms of climate risks, as well as measures to monitor and improve the company's environmental impact (where appropriate).

ii.) Social criteria pertain to an organization's relationships with its employees, supply-chain partners, and the com=munities and countries in which the company is operating.

iii.) Governance criteria pertain to how company performance is led, managed, monitored, and reported. The alignment of these aspects with stakeholder expectations is a crucial factor.

The Organization for Economic Co-operation and Development (OECD) reports that one-fifth of all professionally managed US assets are now invested, at least partially, in environmental, social, and governance principles. While the three pillars are important, the S of the ESG acronym takes center stage. In recent years there has been a 15 percent increase annually across United States companies—and a 10 percent annual increase globally—among survey respondents citing the S of the ESG equation as the most important and significant element to achieving a holistic ESG approach to business success. A 2021 survey done in the UK found that 47 percent of investors considered the S pillar the most important when making decisions, with the E pillar coming in second at 35 percent.[6]

The S is, therefore, important. Failing to address social impacts can damage a company's reputation and, thus, its brand image. This has a direct impact on investors. Companies that are perceived as failing to treat their employees well can experience a significant drop in share price. In some locations, companies that do not adhere to—for instance—inclusion quotas will face regulatory fines. For these reasons, this book is primarily dedicated to the S pillar of the wider ESG equation. The more diverse an enterprise's geography and employee demography, the more critical the S becomes in achieving business success.

A CLOSER LOOK AT S

To develop in an ever-changing world, companies and governments alike must give appropriate attention to the *S* pillar of the ESG equation. In unpacking the *S*, it is helpful to understand what is trying to be achieved.

Throughout the world, some individuals confront barriers that prevent them from fully participating in the economic, social, and political life of the society in which they live. Importantly, this can include the labor market, which is relevant to global businesses. This leaves some people at a disadvantage in their own country. Such disadvantaged individuals can find themselves discriminated against due to age, citizenship status, disability, ethnicity, gender, skin color, religion, and sexual identity or orientation.

In terms of the labor market—and thus the business world— the impact of such discrimination on individuals translates to the loss of earnings and limited employment opportunities. At the national level, the economic cost of social exclusion can be captured by foregone gross domestic product and human capital wealth. Globally, the loss in human capital wealth due to gender inequality alone is estimated to be some $160 trillion.

Social inclusion—be it at the corporate or national level—is the reversal of these kinds of discrimination. It is the application of actions that serve to remove limitations on disadvantaged individuals, enabling them to participate fully in an organization and in society at large. This can be achieved in various ways at both the corporate and national levels, including:

- Provide disadvantaged individuals with the means to express their concerns without fear or shame.

- Enhance access to employment.

- Ensure the distribution of fair opportunities to advance within an organization.

- Promote the participation of disadvantaged individuals in the cultural, social, and political events of the wider community.

SOME INTERESTING EXAMPLES OF SOCIAL-INCLUSION INITIATIVES

The State Department of the United States government maintains several domestic and international programs designed to enhance social inclusion. Its mission statement in this regard is as follows:

> In order to achieve shared prosperity and long-term security in the region, it is essential that all members of our society are able to participate politically, have equal opportunity to participate in economic activity, and have access to education. In every country of the region, historically marginalized groups, including people of African descent, indigenous peoples, lesbian, gay, bisexual, transgender, and intersex (LGBTI) persons, women and girls, youth, and persons with disabilities, confront barriers and discrimination preventing them from fully participating in political, economic, and social life. We work in partnership with civil society, the private sector, and other countries in and outside the region to promote

human rights, social inclusion, inclusive security, and prosperity for all.

On a global scale, the State Department has developed programs with several countries designed to enhance social inclusion in various ways. One example is the US–Brazil Joint Action Plan to Eliminate Racial and Ethnic Discrimination and Promote Equality. This initiative leverages interagency policy expertise in both countries in a unique partnership with civil-society and private-sector committees to address racial health disparities, environmental justice, access to education, equal access to economic opportunities, and the justice system.

The Joint Action Plan recognizes that Brazil and the United States are multiethnic, multiracial democracies whose ties of friendship are strengthened by shared experiences. Both countries celebrate the rich contributions of people of African descent and indigenous populations to the fabric of our societies.

In the corporate world, there are a number of fine examples of specific goals that are being adopted—and actions that are being taken—to enshrine social inclusion into the very structure of the enterprise :

- Accenture maintains specific goals in terms of the number of women in its workforce, as well as target goals related to the hiring of veterans and military spouses. This inclusion initiative has contributed to the company's average annual increase in profits of 15 percent since 2018.[7]

- Diageo has 50 percent female representation on its board and 40 percent on its executive committee.

Diageo has set goals of hitting 40 percent female representation on its senior-leadership team by 2025. Its programs include one covering seventeen countries, which aims to build thriving communities by empowering women. The operating profit of the enterprise more than doubled between 2020 and 2022. Due to Diageo's ongoing inclusion goals, analysts predict this positive profitability trend will continue.[8]

- Gap Inc. maintains business resource groups and advisory boards that are designed to provide opportunities for cultural learning, mentoring, and relationship building among employees. One of the company's programs is devoted to developing an inclusive workforce and a pipeline of future leaders. Apart from a small decline in revenue during the COVID-19 pandemic, the company has enjoyed consistent annual revenue growth since 2017. This positive outlook is partly a reflection of the company's inclusion efforts.[9]

- Medtronic has developed a series of robust diversity networks and employee resource groups for its employees across the globe. Its networks include the African Descent Network, Asian Impact at Medtronic, Hispanic Latino Network, and Medtronic Women's Network. The company's employee resource groups were built to engage employees around shared interests and affinities. This inclusion initiative can be considered a contributing factor to the company's recording an average annual increase in profits of 8 percent in the period between 2020 to 2021.[10]

Although these examples pertain to large companies, social-inclusion practices can be adopted at even the smallest companies. It serves business owners to apply these practices from the get-go to develop a culture of inclusion that sets the business up for success in the long term. Companies of all sizes that embed social-inclusion metrics into their operations enjoy better communication and engagement with their entire group of stakeholders.

Company performance can thus be directly aligned with social metrics, with the results soon measurable. Such essential factors include:

- Enhanced employee engagement is an immediate benefit following the implementation of a social-inclusion program. This automatically brings the additional benefit of a lower employee turnover rate.

- Socially inclusive enterprises are 21 percent more likely to enjoy enhanced profitability than competing companies that have not embraced social inclusion.[11]

- The implementation of a socially inclusive recruitment strategy results in a wider pool of talent available to recruiters. Many job seekers prioritize companies that maintain social-inclusion programs.

- Social inclusion results in diverse team structures. This, in turn, delivers heightened levels of innovation to an organization.

THE CULTURAL ELEMENT

Within the context of the *S* in ESG, cultural intelligence is a very important element. As we have already observed, the assumed cultural norms of any given country are becoming less and less relevant. Our ever-changing globalized world causes more and more individuals to possess their cultural characteristics, due to either their heritage or simply their own life story. This makes understanding the cultural component of social inclusion all the more critical and—simultaneously—all the more complex and fascinating.

Cultural intelligence (CQ) in the workplace is vital to bottom-line business success. Experienced global CEOs recognize that CQ impacts strategy, brand, sales, and operational performance. It is, however, the element that many business leaders often overlook. Cultural competencies must be learned in order to even know how to recognize, acknowledge, and respect others and the way in which work gets done in other countries. This is becoming ever more important as workplaces become increasingly remote and global.

In subsequent chapters of this book, we will closely examine the specificities of cultural intelligence and cultural competencies. Before we do that, we want to recognize that we all see the world through our own cultural lens, which is made up of so many facets of our lives. We don't wake up in the morning and intuitively know that where and how we grew up has made us see the world through our unique lens.

Chapter 4

CULTURAL AWARENESS: KNOWING ONESELF

BECOMING AWARE OF CULTURAL AWARENESS

Knowing one's own cultural propensity in terms of such dimensions as communication, hierarchy, and relationships has an enormous impact on success, for it is only when we conduct a study of our own assumptions and biases that we can understand those of a different culture. It should be noted that our cultural propensity comes not only from the country in which we are born but from all our life experiences. A British national who has been living in France for twenty years, for example, no longer has the cultural profile of someone who has never left the United Kingdom. Once we know our cultural profile through a digital cultural assessment, we can then invite managers to conduct the same assessment procedure for colleagues and team members. In this way, managers can observe the characteristics that they may share with—and those that may diverge from—team members either directly in their office or in a remote location. Leaders can build a cultural map of a team or an entire organization, providing a clear vision of any potential cultural challenges as they lead and grow the organization.

Cultural intelligence has become so relevant because it is difficult to imagine any organization today operating without some element of global interaction. Companies are augmenting their service delivery model to be available to clients 24/7. Furthermore, global supply and value chains increasingly operate across borders. To that end, corporations are building ever more geographically distributed teams to enhance their capabilities to support growth. As a result, employees are increasingly working across multiple time zones and national cultures.

This workplace shift has led to fundamental changes in how work gets done. As teams become more global, they lose their shared assumptions and norms. Human interaction becomes significantly more complex. Because they do not work in the same physical space as some of their colleagues, employees need to learn new collaboration skills while developing a better understanding of cultural differences.

As organizations become more global, there is a need to better support leaders and employees who work across multiple time zones and national cultures. The goal is for organizations to prepare global leaders to operate more effectively across cultures while leading global teams. Global teams also need to work effectively across borders. As these skills improve, significant synergies can emerge, which effectively bring the best of all cultures to the organization as a whole.

For example, a US-based company moved a segment of work to another country without considering that the two work teams had never worked together. Issues became evident as processes and team interactions became ineffective. Leaders correctly assessed that the root of much of the problem stemmed from cultural differences, such as attitudes about time, interaction with authority, and sensitivity to dissenting opinions. To address this issue, leaders created a change-management plan to build cross-cultural awareness so that employees from these teams could more effectively collaborate. As a result, the teams experienced greater mutual understanding and improved interaction.

Cross-cultural management takes significant time, effort, and energy. Global leaders have direct responsibilities for teams working across multiple countries and time zones. Therefore, they need to understand the importance of having a global frame of reference while preserving local relevance. Everyday decision-making and communications are more complex for global leaders. Global leaders, for example, need to decide which key messages are shared and how those messages are communicated. They might need to decide where and when to hold "town halls" and which technology is more conducive to communicating with geographically dispersed work teams.

UNDERSTANDING THE PRIMARY BARRIERS

Different definitions of time

People in certain cultures tend to look at time as a fixed concept, while people from other cultures tend to view time as fluid. Inconsistent attitudes toward time can lead to cost overruns in projects. For example, employees working for the Brazilian division of a US-based company may react negatively to mandatory overtime because they perceive time-measured deliverables to be flexible and hence view the overtime differently than their US counterparts. Of all the impacts of cross-cultural interaction, this one aspect may be the most easily noticeable at the onset of working together.

Direct versus indirect communication

In cultures that are more content-driven, communication tends to be direct and explicit, with a focus on speaking concisely. Meaning is found in the words. Conversely, in context-driven cultures, communication is more indirect and implicit, with messages that are read "between the lines." Meaning is found around the words. Indian nationals, for example, are often asked, "What's up with the Indian nod?" The best explanation is that it means: "I heard you." It communicates neither a yes nor a no. Sometimes, the nod is a polite way of saying no, when doing so openly might put the relationship at risk. Additionally, people from different cultures often have a sense of pace when they communicate. Email communications are an integral part of our workplace. However, acceptable response times often vary greatly. Typically, within the United States there is an unwritten rule to respond promptly. This approach may not be the norm in other cultures.

Differing attitudes toward hierarchy

Certain cultures tend to be more hierarchical and directive, while others tend to be more participative or collaborative. A human resources business partner experienced this cultural dimension after relocating from India to the United States. She was very quiet during a meeting with her manager and a senior leader in the organization. After the meeting, her manager offered some feedback. He started by saying something positive (a common

US approach to offering feedback). Then, he mentioned that she did not speak during the meeting. A bit puzzled by his comment, she replied that she was waiting for him to invite her to speak.

Building and defining relationships

People in some cultures tend to lead with the task, and then, in the process of doing the job, they build relationships. Other cultures are more relationship-focused. People tend to lead by building relationships and then getting the task done. For example, if managers dive into the task with employees in certain Middle Eastern cultures, they may have a very polite conversation, but the work may not get done. In some parts of the world, teams cannot get to work immediately. Instead, they must first focus on the relationship because it is the way they build trust and credibility.

UNDERSTANDING THE IMPORTANCE OF CULTURAL AWARENESS

When asked about the importance of cross-cultural awareness, a global team leader across multiple countries suggested, "It is important to be aware of current affairs in a location—greetings, customs, festivals or holidays, and other events. People in different cultures have a different sense of time and a different commitment level to when and how they work. Organizational hierarchy may be different from culture to culture. It is important to pick up on body language and nonverbal elements of communication."

An interesting comparison is that of an iceberg, which is primarily invisible below the water. Like icebergs, culture centers around intrinsic values and beliefs "hidden" beneath the surface.

Those same values and beliefs shape culture's extrinsic side: how people think and behave. Several cultural dimensions come into play when developing cultural awareness. These dimensions are the binary ends of the spectrum. While cultural dimensions inform our thinking and help us understand cultural differences, they do not define cultures and people. Cross-cultural awareness and communication norms remain key competencies for effective leadership in global organizations. Leaders and employees must develop these competencies in order to work effectively in cross-cultural environments.

The following chapters of this book describe the nine key cultural dimensions that can be considered the ingredients of a national "norm." Among these chapters are some personal accounts of those who have experienced cultures outside their own. These testify to the truth that culture is not a static thing. It evolves in and of itself, and in the life stories of those around us. In other words, the awareness of the cultural environment surrounding each team member is only part of the equation. The critical element in achieving team cohesion is the ability to fully understand the individuals that make up the team.

Chapter 5

A PERSONAL JOURNEY OF CULTURE AND INCLUSION

By Erika Mercedes, Diversity Business Leader at
a Fortune 50 Social Technology Company

EACH OF OUR STORIES IS complex and multidimensional, influenced by our struggles and experiences. Growing up, my experiences were heavily influenced by my family and culture. I was raised speaking both English and Spanish at home, I have a deep appreciation for self-expression through Latin music and food, and I learned to value the wisdom and experience of my elders very early on. I grew up in an environment that valued relationships, open communication, respect, and hard work to progress toward a life better than that of those who came before me. My grandparents had left the lives they knew in Puerto Rico to come to cities in the mainland United States, where they did not speak the language and would work third-shift factory jobs in order to provide for their families. They took risks and leaned on a community of other family members to survive. Neither of my grandparents had the privilege of advanced education or college degrees, but with grit they were able to make progress, purchase homes, and raise their families in loving communities.

When I think of my identity and how it has been influenced, I realize that I often consider myself an "in-betweener" across many dimensions of culture in my life. My passion for inclusion has been with me from a very young age. Even as a young child, I valued difference and was curious about its complexities. I do not believe that our identities are defined at a specific point of origin or have a set destination but instead believe that they continuously flow in an evolutionary phase, influenced by our experiences and life changes. Culture most certainly ties in with identity, and the complexity of trying to balance multiple cultures has played a significant role in my own identity and my lifestyle.

For me, college was a very transformative experience that prompted a more profound journey of self-discovery. I went to a predominantly white college, and that was a new environment for me. I was the first in my family to leave home to attend a four-year college, the first in my family to study abroad, and the first to pursue a corporate career. My family has always been supportive of me; however, there was only sometimes a shared understanding of my experiences.

Through these experiences, I became much more aware of my "otherness." I am so grateful because those experiences sparked my interest in social justice and inclusion. The struggles, mistakes, and discomfort I sometimes felt prompted me to learn more about my own identity and cultural history. It was during my first corporate internship that I first heard about the "unspoken playbook." I was really fortunate to receive mentorship from a leader who helped me navigate that first corporate adventure. I admired Judy's brilliance and her ability to connect with others in the most thoughtful way. She challenged me that summer and took the time to teach me skills that I would not learn in the classroom. She introduced me to those unspoken "rules," the knowledge of which is necessary to navigate traditional corporate environments and advance careers. As a first-generation college student, I did not know how to influence and leverage a network, navigate workplace politics, or even advocate for myself.

Over the next several years, I spent countless hours observing, seeking mentorship, and learning the "rules" of the workplace. I invested an unbelievable amount of energy in trying to assimilate and adjust to fit a stereotypical profile of a successful young professional. I saw some success in this process, but, as I progressed in my career and the workplace started to shift generationally, I began to realize that I needed to define my own story.

Trying to consistently follow a map not created by me or reflecting my multidimensional identity seemed quite a heavy load to bear. For first- and second-generation US Americans, there are often expectations to conform to your specific cultures. While assimilating to the "American" identity, you also need to meet the traditional standards of your other cultures. Cultures serve as identifiers in society, influencing the clothes we wear, the foods we eat, the languages we speak, and the values we practice. Yet, they can serve as barriers to as much as help with cultivating character.

I've developed the capacity to adjust my working style so as to thrive in different spaces and connect with others without necessarily abandoning any one aspect of my identity. I can still be authentic but, at the same time, thoughtful of how I show up. I am a woman, I am a Latina, I am a mom, I am a wife, I am a daughter, I am a millennial professional, and I am an activist for inclusion, among many other things. And *all* of these roles may show up differently at different stages of my life. I believe that the many dimensions of our identities are our superpowers. On numerous occasions, I have been the only one—the only female, the only Latina, the only millennial. The rules are different then, and the reality is that there are different playbooks for other people, often influenced by a level of privilege. At various points in my career and in the communities in which I have lived, I have felt that I have needed to be extraordinary to succeed and belong. It can be exhausting.

The complexities of culture carry on from one generation to the next. The Latino culture has heavily influenced who I am, but there are also other traditions and norms that I have adopted as my own. My mixed cultural identity has allowed me to bring unique perspectives and ideas that advance my personal and professional life. It has encouraged me to engage in difficult conversations about race, gender, and privilege. It is what drives me to focus on inclusion work. Multigenerational diversity in the workforce is also challenging communication styles, identity, choice and control of how we work, and aspirations for more equitable and inclusive workplaces. As the future of work continues to evolve, the rules need to evolve as well.

As I reflect on this, I recognize that I may lean more toward one style or identity based on my own cultural upbringing and experiences. Still, I must continuously flex new muscles to understand and effectively work in a more-connected global world. Through my journey of self-discovery and identity, I have learned that individuals who possess a high level of cultural intelligence play an important role in bridging divides and knowledge gaps in an organization: educating peers about different cultures; transferring knowledge between otherwise disparate groups; helping to build interpersonal connections and smooth interpersonal processes in a multicultural workforce. Cultural intelligence also drives innovation and creativity by integrating multiple perspectives and diverse resources.

Yet, cultural competency is not necessarily one of the "unspoken playbook" chapters. Although some may naturally possess a high level of cultural competency through rich lived experience, many of us need to develop this skill. When we seek to understand and learn how cultural norms influence behavior, we can unlock new potential and connect with others more effectively. I will admit that I have undergone hard lessons in cultural competency while navigating global roles.

Several years back, when leading the rollout of a global program, I facilitated a virtual meeting with a team based in the UK to review the rollout plan of an inclusion curriculum (the irony). I had detailed each step of the process for the team, and, in my mind, the rollout would require minimal effort and time given that we had already widely rolled out the program in the US. However, I was met with resistance and intimidation from my colleagues. Even after several subsequent conversations, I needed help to get the necessary buy-in and support. I felt frustrated and stressed, as deadlines were quickly approaching. Had I missed some details? Was I not being assertive enough in my approach? Why wasn't the team prioritizing a program that was being supported by top leadership? Did the team have a personal issue with me? There were so many questions that I was grappling with, yet I was struggling to find answers. Although I had interacted with the team on video calls and virtual forums on numerous occasions, I had never met several of the team members in person. I knew that I needed the support of the team to execute the program. Under pressure, I decided to visit the office to obtain buy-in from the group and discuss the next steps in person. Before meeting with the broader team, I decided to have a candid conversation with the business leaders and ask my questions. Within a short time, I realized that I had failed to recognize the cultural differences that were serving as barriers and were critically important to driving the work.

I had not cultivated relationships and taken the time to listen to the needs of the team; the terminology and the approach for the project did not resonate with the UK team; and I had not considered some of the team dynamics that would impact the work. Over the next several days and weeks, I took the time to get to know the key players that would drive the job, listened to the perspectives of and feedback from the core team, and created the space to challenge how we were working. I had been trying to implement a program that was designed by a US team for a US audience and that did not take into consideration key cultural dimensions of our global teams. We adjusted the timeline as needed and decided to develop a custom program that would resonate. As a result, I was able to get additional engagement from team members in the UK, and we started to see even more progress and impact than the program had in the US.

As a first-generation professional, learning the unspoken rules of the playbook in the workplace has provided me with many valuable lessons. I also learned that one of the most important aspects of those lessons is recognizing when to break the rules and forge your own trail. There are many paths to success. Sometimes those rules create limits that do not fit today's changing global world and our multidimensional identities. Communicating and interacting with people across cultures helps us work well with others while also aiding us on our journey of self-discovery.

My journey to develop cultural competence has required reflection and self-awareness to understand who I am and what I bring to relationships and situations. Through this process, I continue to learn about my evolving social identity and cultural influences and how those intersect. It has required me to get uncomfortable, to be curious, and to empathize. Our social identities affect our interpersonal, communication, and work styles, as well as our views of equity, conflict, hierarchy, leadership, and sense of time (among many others). Cultural competence is an ongoing process that ultimately fosters more creative problem-solving, aids in becoming better listeners and communicators, improves adaptability, and provides a genuine foundation for driving sustainable equity and inclusion.

Chapter 6

THE CULTURAL DIMENSION OF TIME

KNOWING OTHERS

Cultures around the world all have different relationships with the concept of time. The dimension of time refers to whether people view time as something that can be bought and controlled or as something that is fluid. Many cultures believe that time is uncontrollable. These cultures have a low level of time sensitivity. People do not get annoyed when others are late. Being late does not demonstrate a lack of respect; it does not reflect on the person's character or ability to organize life, nor does it hold any meaning about the person's attitude toward the one who was kept waiting. Time is viewed as an element beyond one's control, much like the weather. In a low-time culture, people will be more concerned about people's feelings than about adhering to a schedule. Meetings sometimes don't begin on time, but people will use the time they are waiting to strengthen relationships and build networks.

Cultures that are less sensitive to time are usually high on the relationship scale. In these cultures, it is important to allow plenty of room for networking and relationship building. This time spent together will improve the overall relationships and the collaboration for future projects as well. I often work with leaders from high-time cultures like the US and Germany that don't believe it's important to allocate time in the business day to build relationships. They usually bring me in later on when the project or business is failing to help them unpack what has gone wrong. It's always because they didn't build those relationships. In low-time and even some high-time cultures like Japan, credibility, respect, and trust are built through the relationship. You either spend the time upfront to ensure success or pay later when the project is failing.

BEST PRACTICE FOR MANAGERS IN LOW-TIME CULTURES

Countries with a low-time context will ignore time passing if a conversation is unfinished. Individuals from such countries will feel offended if relationship-building is not part of the dialogue. Adequate time must be allowed when scheduling important meetings or giving feedback so that the person receiving it feels valued. The person giving the feedback must be flexible about when the session ends. Building esteem by pointing out what the individual is doing well is an essential developmental input for this group. In addition, take care to note improvements. Talk earnestly with the person about improving and discuss their ideas to develop a way forward.

- Conversations should be started informally to build trust and rapport. The other person or persons involved should be asked for their opinion on how things are going. Build time into your meeting to do this, as it will be better to have extra time scheduled than to be rushed.

- Positive feedback should be given regularly and informally rather than waiting for a meeting.

- A rapport should be established before giving any developmental feedback. Be empathetic and attempt to understand. The conversation may be more extended than you would prefer but taking the time to do so will build a better relationship.

- Feedback should be planned, although the conversation may occur differently than expected.

- Time frames and milestones should be set. In low-time cultures, meeting deadlines can be a challenge. Dates should therefore be confirmed and followed up on more often than you might typically do.

BEST PRACTICE FOR MANAGERS IN HIGH-TIME CULTURES

In cultures where time is viewed as a commodity, it should be spent wisely. Individuals in high-time countries value regular, planned meetings and have set expectations for what will occur. They will feel undervalued if a prearranged feedback session does not take place on schedule. They may think that "time is money," so be sure to keep feedback short, specific, and easy to act on.

Individuals in high-time cultures expect feedback in a structured and timely way, presented with direct developmental points. They will not appreciate a large amount of "small talk" before receiving feedback, as this can be perceived as a waste of time and even as a sign of disrespect. Feedback should be impact driven and delivered explicitly.

- Regular one-on-one meetings should be set. The time allocated should be entirely dedicated to regular ongoing and specific feedback.

- Developmental input should be planned in advance and then delivered with clear action points. Check for understanding and keep the conversation short and direct.

- Positive feedback should be delivered succinctly and regularly.

KNOWING YOURSELF—TIME

The two scenarios below relate to the cultural dimension of time. The most natural response to each indicates where one may fall on the time-dimension scale. There is no right or wrong answer. Individuals may find themselves in a place on the scale different than what is the cultural norm for their home country. This may be due to having lived in countries other than their country of origin or to having other influences within the country of origin. It may also be due to having experienced a working environment different from the origin country's cultural norms.

Scenario 1

You work for a large global enterprise, and you are preparing for a coworker event including participants from all over the world.

Response A: You suggest to your manager that the event should be scheduled over two days with plenty of networking time between sessions. The participants seldom meet in person, but they do all know each other a little. You believe that the time will improve future collaboration.

Response B: You feel great because you have been able to fit all the conference subjects into the full agenda. Your schedule begins at eight o'clock in the morning and ends at five o'clock in the evening with a thirty-minute lunch break and two fifteen-minute coffee breaks in the morning and afternoon.

In reviewing the responses, it can be concluded that individuals and cultures with low time sensitivities would favor Response A. Conversely, in high-time cultures, Response B is more appropriate.

Scenario 2

You are a manager, and you are faced with a conflict. John complains about Dennis chitchatting with coworkers and ignoring deadlines on an internal project.

Response A: You ask for Dennis's side of the story. Dennis apologizes for the untimely deliveries but points out that the "small talk" with coworkers revealed unknown and valid flaws in the project. You agree that solving the project correctly is more important than the deadline.

Response B: You ask Dennis to account for his hours over the last four weeks. You reprimand Dennis for not delivering on the deadline.

A manager in a low-time cultural environment should attempt to stay open-minded toward time sensitivity and educate herself by learning the cultural competencies to flex to get the desired performance results.

Response A would therefore be more appropriate.

Response B applies in high-time cultures. When projects do have critical deadlines, managers should pursue organized and more frequent communication methods for essential issues that surface.

KNOWING YOUR TEAM—TIME

Now that you know more about how you think about time culturally, let's look at a few case studies and scenarios to see how this shows up on teams.

Leslie (High-Time-Orientation US American)

Leslie has been with Kelowna Foods for three years and is settling into her new role as sales manager for the Americas. She has responsibility for the entire continent, from Canada in the north to Argentina in the south. Leslie has been given a specific set of goals for the year ahead by her US-based company. As this is her first year in the role, she is anxious to meet—or even exceed—the expectations of the C-suite. She is confident in her ability to deliver given that she has consistently achieved her sales goals in the domestic roles that she has previously held.

Luis (Low-Time-Orientation Mexican National)

Luis reports to Leslie as the national sales manager for Mexico, the company's largest market in Latin America, and one with consistently high sales. He is a knowledgeable and capable leader with years of experience in the food industry. He had a good relationship with the previous regional manager, but he has not worked with Leslie for very long and has few expectations about her style.

TIME

LOW — − − − | − − | − | + | + + | + + + — HIGH

Luis   Leslie

Scenario

Luis received an email from his leader, Leslie, asking for feedback on proposed regional meeting dates. While it seemed interesting, he was focused on an essential sales pitch and was prepping his team for a customer presentation. This deal would ensure that they met their sales goals, and then some. He meant to respond and was surprised when Leslie called him to express her displeasure at his lack of reply. She sounded angry and upset.

Luis was surprised by her reactions and thought she was overreacting. Clearly, Leslie did not understand how important the sales pitch was to the company. He told her that he would respond but had not had time to review the dates. Now it seems as though he is on the wrong side of his boss, and that has him worried.

What are some actions Luis could take to improve the situation?

1. Look at his personal preferences regarding time.

   Luis has a low time sensitivity and those people will often focus on numerous things simultaneously. Luis needs to understand his own cultural tendencies in order to flex to create a better working relationship with Leslie.

2. Consider the national cultural dimensions of his new leader.

   Luis uses the cultural assessment tool to review preferences for the US. He learns that US colleagues are high on this dimension and more driven by deadlines. They will not appreciate an extended amount of time to return an email or a phone call.

   Likely, Leslie will also expect to get feedback on plans and initiatives during the meeting, delivered directly. In contrast, Luis's colleagues in Latin America are from a low-time culture. They will likely view the videoconference as an excellent opportunity to network and connect with personal stories and chitchat. The various sales managers seldom get to see each other. They believe that the time spent together (albeit virtually) will improve the group's collaboration and enhance everyone's chances of success.

3. Understand and acknowledge Leslie's feedback.

Luis needs to respond to the situation and explain to Leslie that he sees things differently and, at the moment, had different priorities. He needs to let her know that the meeting is a priority for him. While he should ask for feedback and for guidance on her expectations going forward, he should also provide feedback to her on the way she responded. Having an honest and open conversation about the situation will help them to move forward and prevent bad feelings and resentment in the future.

4. Consider the time dimension of culture.

Luis has learned that Leslie values time and expects deadlines to be met. This style is a slightly different way of working than he is used to, so he will need to flex to succeed. Discussing the dimension of time will help Leslie see that his culture differs from hers. There are many ways to incorporate both sides of this dimension into meetings so that all participants can benefit.

When possible, flex to align with the time preferences of your team. Low-time-orientation cultures will need and expect extra time to talk through plans and actions, giving feedback as trust develops; high-time cultures will appreciate more-concise meetings and calls. They will more readily give feedback and expect to receive it without having a strong need to build a relationship.

KNOWING WHERE

The dimension of time around the world:

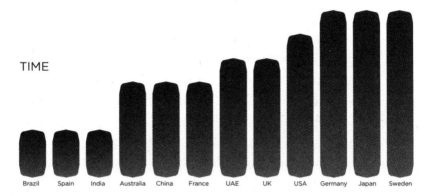

TIME

Brazil Spain India Australia China France UAE UK USA Germany Japan Sweden

LOW   **HIGH**

Chapter 7

THE CULTURAL DIMENSION OF RELATIONSHIPS

THIS DIMENSION DESCRIBES THE VALUE placed on relationships between people in life and in business. Some cultures assign a relatively low value to relationships. Others view relationships as the basis for building trust, credibility, and respect. This is called the trust equation.

Low-relationship cultures such as the US and Germany tend to rely heavily on legal systems and penalties to protect rights, as opposed to expecting that the trust between individuals compels them to act honestly and fairly in business and social transactions. In these cultures, a long-term development may be three months. However, in cultures like Japan and China, relationships are more highly regarded and *long-term* may refer to periods of three decades or longer.

In cultures that value relationships, you must trust someone to work comfortably with them, which is critical to business. Knowing the people you work with is as necessary as respecting their professional credentials. On the other hand, in a culture with low sensitivity to relationships, doing business in person may be considered overkill. These cultures are more transactional, and they just want to get the job done and seldom seek to know the people with whom they do business.

In high-relationship cultures, mutual trust is critical in business, and the business decision-making cycle is slower. High-relationship cultures value long-term business friendships and partnerships, while low-relationship cultures are readily comfortable with conducting business dealings primarily by email. In low-relationship cultures, getting to know someone outside the business setting is usually considered irrelevant to the business.

Not understanding the importance of relationships and how trust is built are the main reasons most leaders fail when they take on a new position in another country or begin leading a global team. I recently coached a senior executive at a major pharmaceutical company. When I met her, she had just left a key position at one of the largest pharma companies in the world. I had been told that she had left suddenly, and it wasn't positive. I asked her what happened.

She said, "I didn't take the time to build the credit in the bank before I tried to cash it in."

I said to her, "So you didn't build relationships. Why not?"

She said, "I grew up speaking French and had worked in Paris for ten years when my company transferred me to Montreal. I thought it would be the same culture as France."

What she didn't realize was that the Quebecois are less hierarchical than the Parisians, but they are still high on the relationship scale.

I asked her, "Why didn't you take the time to build relationships?"

She said, "In Paris, they would have done the work and embraced me because of my title because it's a more hierarchical culture than Montreal." By the time she needed her team to work with her, it was too late. She said they felt disrespected and slighted and from that moment they worked against her, and it never changed. She said it was the worst time of her career.

BEST PRACTICE FOR MANAGERS IN LOW-RELATIONSHIP CULTURES

In low-relationship-oriented cultures, feedback is direct and quantifiable. Performance evaluations are task-based rather than personal. The message's clarity is crucial.

The feedback recipient tends not to take criticism personally. The feedback is likely to be discussed, including any areas of contention. The successful delivery of feedback in low-relationship cultures often includes a measurable action plan, which monitors the ongoing progress of the recipient.

- Positive feedback should be kept brief.
- Developmental feedback should focus on the task or behavior. Too many personal or small-talk comments are not necessary.
- Facts and metrics should be used.
- An action plan should be prepared in advance, highlighting ways to improve.
- Follow-up meetings or calls to check progress should be set. These should be data-based.

BEST PRACTICE FOR MANAGERS IN HIGH-RELATIONSHIP CULTURES

As already observed, high-relationship cultures value relationships as investments, making them a key to long-term business success. Whatever the business context, it is not appropriate to give feedback in a way that may offend or cause a lack of trust.

Direct negative feedback can lead to a loss of face and embarrassment for the receiver. When the enterprise's success revolves around the team rather than the individual, people do not want to feel that they have let the team down. The recipient may not feel inclined to discuss the given feedback in such cultures.

If someone from a culture where directness is the norm delivers feedback, a change in communication style will be required. First and foremost, strive to maintain a positive relationship and uphold the reputation of the person receiving the feedback. Being less direct, softening one's tone, and using empathy and positive body language are good ways to begin. Successful feedback in high-relationship cultures requires the discussion of alternatives and options rather than direct criticism of the employee.

- An action plan should be prepared.
- The feedback recipient should be told that they are a valuable team member and why you think so.
- Developmental feedback should focus on the behavior, not the person. Give specific examples of desired outcomes. Build esteem while providing guidance.
- It is advisable to be cautious about criticizing or using accusatory language. Instead of asking, "Why did you do this?" request context for the situation.

State that you would like to hear their perspective and understand the problem.

- Open-ended questions should be asked. Rapport should be built throughout the conversation, and ideas for improvement should be developed.

- It is necessary to continue to check in and to coach the person to the desired performance.

KNOWING YOURSELF—RELATIONSHIPS

The three scenarios below relate to the cultural dimension of relationships. The most natural response to each indicates where one may fall on the relationships-dimension scale. There is no right or wrong answer. Individuals may find themselves in a place on the scale different than the cultural norm of their home country. This may be due to having lived in countries other than or had other influences within their country of origin. It may also be due to having experienced a working environment different from the origin country's cultural norms.

Scenario 1

You have been promoted to the role of product manager for the software company you joined two months ago. Your immediate task is to collect client feedback on the company's latest software application. The application is costly and is sold globally to large enterprises.

Response A: You look up the client in your CRM system and call the contact. As a follow-up to the call, you email the contact an online questionnaire.

Response B: You decide that to get high-quality feedback and build trust, it is essential to visit your clients in person.

Response A is appropriate for low-relationship cultures. The clients operate in a culture with low sensitivity to relationships, so an in-person visit is considered a waste of money. The product manager can plan a budget and timeline accordingly.

In high-relationship cultures, an in-person meeting is always the way to go. In that case, response B is the appropriate strategy.

Scenario 2

You need to renew the reseller agreement with your Asia-Pacific resellers. You have managed the APAC resellers for less than a year. How do you handle this challenge?

Response A: You email the resellers and attach the new agreement. You ask them all to join an online Q&A session. You prefer this efficient approach.

Response B: You worry that the APAC resellers will find it suspicious if you email them the agreement without any warning. Your budget does not allow for an in-person trip, but you compromise by setting up individual videoconference calls with each reseller's CEO and carefully planning each call's agenda.

Low-relationship cultures have low expectations in terms of the level of attention and contact necessary in ongoing business dealings. Response A would generally apply here.

In high-relationship cultures, an enhanced level of personal contact provides an invaluable opportunity to better understand those involved and achieve business success. Therefore, Response B would be more appropriate in such locations.

Scenario 3

> You just started to work for a start-up. The start-up relies heavily on some critical investors based in South America, and it is essential that you secure certain key people's support for a new product. You visit the investors in person.
>
> **Response A:** You ask the supporters to sign a nondisclosure agreement (NDA) prior to your arrival. For those who sign the NDA, you schedule a two-hour presentation. After the presentation, you expect them to sign a legal statement that confirms their support.
>
> **Response B:** You spend a day with each key supporter and shake hands in friendship. You will reach out to them later in the week in a personal phone call to ask them to sign the legal statement.

Low-relationship cultures are more transactional than high-relationship cultures. The goal is to get the job done rather than knowing everything about the business partners. Response A is, therefore, more appropriate in such cultures.

Response B is the right way to go in high-relationship cultures. In such locations, it is imperative to trust business partners.

KNOWING TEAM COLLEAGUES

Understanding the differences between the low and high orientation of relationships in global team situations.

Team Members

Shuzo (High-Relationship-Orientation
Japanese National)

Shuzo is a senior manager based in Tokyo. He has worked for Lotus Enterprises for many years, and Green Chemicals is now acquiring the company. He is from Japan, having studied and spent his entire career there. He is very proud of his high tenure with the company and is loyal to the firm. Shuzo manages a large team and trusts them. His team is nervous about the acquisition and worried about job security and work styles.

Doug (Low-Relationship-Orientation
US American)

Doug is a manager working for Green Chemicals. He works at the global headquarters in Houston, Texas. He is known for his straightforward communication style and his ability to get things done. Due to the retirement of his long-serving predecessor, Doug has just been promoted and given responsibility for the Northeast Asia region. Although he has not worked directly with this region before, he knows many people in that office. To meet his goals, he will need to manage the acquisition and get the new office in Japan on board.

RELATIONSHIP

Doug   **Shuzo**

Scenario

Green's acquisition of the Asian enterprise is final, and Doug now manages employees from both organizations. Shuzo, the company's regional manager for Northeast Asia, is in Japan. Doug is anxious to build his relationship with Shuzo, despite their geography and cultural differences.

How does Doug achieve this?

1. Understand his own and the team's cultural preferences regarding relationships.

   Doug completes his profile to measure where he is on the relationship-dimension scale and asks Shuzo to do the same. The results show that he and Shuzo are at opposite ends. Their profiles help Doug better understand what he needs to do moving forward to ensure that the development of his relationship with Shuzo is optimized and, therefore, more likely to be successful.

2. Understand the cultural dimensions of both countries.

   Doug's next step is to look at the cultural differences between the United States and Japan regarding relationships. The United States assigns a low value to business relationships, relying on its legal system to protect contracts and transactions. In Japan, the long-term building of relationships is an integral part of any and all business activity.

3. Align relationship preferences.

   The cultural-profiling exercise made Doug aware that he needed to gain Shuzo's trust by building a relationship, which he could not do through a phone call. Doug factors in several business trips between the United States and Japan when planning his budget. For the first year of their relationship, Doug budgets for him and Shuzo to visit in person once a quarter, alternating the traveling between the two.

   When planning these trips, Doug remembers to add extra time to the itinerary for socializing. He also establishes an ongoing schedule of video calls between him and Shuzo—on a more frequent basis than he has with his other team members in the region. During his meetings with Shuzo, Doug makes an effort to share personal information about his life outside of work. He finds that they both enjoy golf and plans a more casual "walking meeting" at a golf course in Japan during his next trip to allow more time to build a relationship with Shuzo.

Look for ways to connect on topics outside of work with those in high-relationship cultures. Topics could include family, sports, hobbies, and other interests.

4. Flex the style of giving feedback.

When Doug needs to provide feedback to Shuzo, he should flex his rather direct style. He will want to focus developmental input on tasks and desired outcomes, not on personal habits. Shuzo may be embarrassed by developmental feedback and, as a result, shut down or decline to ask any questions.

Plan feedback carefully and provide specific steps and actions so as to meet desired outcomes. Watch for nonverbal reactions to feedback.

If one cannot give feedback in person, make sure to take extra time to explain what didn't go well and outline what needs to change. Allow time for questions. End on a positive note and build esteem by letting the person know that you value their work. Plan specific follow-up meetings to check their progress. Knowing your style and that of the feedback receiver helps you flex your style to be more effective.

5. Encourage and build a feedback culture.

Over time, Doug and Shuzo can build a good working relationship. Doug sets regular one-on-one meetings and rarely cancels. They spend time during the meetings reviewing outcomes, and Doug is mindful to ask Shuzo what feedback he has and the support he needs. Building a feedback culture gives Doug a better understanding of what is happening in Japan, and he grows to rely on Shuzo as a trusted partner.

When working with high-relationship cultures, understand that building the relationship is essential to doing business. You will be unlikely to receive feedback until there is trust, and feedback given may be taken in silence.

KNOWING WHERE

The dimension of relationships around the world:

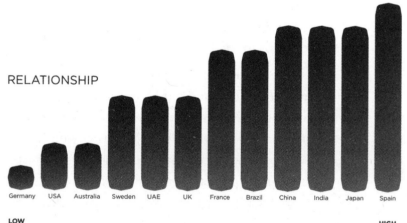

RELATIONSHIP

Germany USA Australia Sweden UAE UK France Brazil China India Japan Spain

LOW   **HIGH**

Low-Relationship Culture

A country with one of the lowest-relationship cultures in the world is Australia.

Some Cultural Etiquette Observations for Australian Business Settings

In business settings, the atmosphere is predominantly relaxed. Despite this, one should always arrive on time for a business meeting. Tardiness and unannounced visits are frowned upon. Australians will most often take a direct approach in business dealings and appreciate brevity. Long-winded speeches or meetings are ill-advised. However, before a meeting, one should take time for a limited amount of general discussion. Allowing some time to make a personal connection before the business negotiation starts is usually appreciated. A firm handshake and direct eye contact in Australia is an appropriate greeting.

High-Relationship Culture

A country with one of the highest-relationship cultures in the world is Japan.

Some Cultural Etiquette Observations for Japanese Business Settings

The long history of tradition and respect is apparent in the Japanese belief in the connection between age and rank. Always show the utmost respect to the oldest person in the gathering or setting. Elders are considered a pillar of the culture.

Formality is not only a tradition in Japan but a form of respect, whether addressing someone or receiving a business card. One should use *san* and the person's last name unless invited to do otherwise. The word *san* is a form of *Mr.* or

Mrs. If offered a business card, it is considered disrespectful to place it immediately in one's wallet or pocket. During a business conversation, one should be mindful of respecting the physical distance between others. As the country is also at the high end of the space-dimension scale, the Japanese may prefer to have more physical space between their business counterparts than do some other cultures.

While most westerners might be uncomfortable with silence, it is not the same for the Japanese. This culture views silence as a valuable and generative practice. Public displays of affection between men and women—single or married—are not appropriate in Japan.

Bowing is a traditional form of greeting others in Japan. The depth of the bow is representative of the relationship status. Correct bowing involves closing the eyes and placing the palms at one's thighs. The Japanese are very familiar with Western culture, so one may receive a handshake. The handshake may be less firm than is the norm in many Western countries.

Vignette: My Multicultural Career Experiences:
A Journey from Europe to China,
the Mediterranean, and the United States

*By Giancarlo Francese, Scientist and Senior
Pharma Executive, United States*

I was born to a French mother and an Italian father in the small country of Belgium (one of the initial founding countries of the European Union). I then grew up primarily in Italy. As such, cultural immersion has always been pivotal to my understanding of how to approach daily life within different life perspectives and historical and cultural backgrounds. I learned to respect different cultures, listen, observe, and understand rather than make fast and superficial judgments and move away from the unconscious and conscious biases that are barriers to creating and developing healthy relationships. I always strive to build a multicultural career in different countries and continents. In other words, I aim to constantly learn and appreciate the beauty and incredible achievements that are the benefits of an inclusive work and life environment.

Upon concluding my studies in Italy, I gained my first job experience in Zürich, which is one of the Swiss German-speaking cantons of Switzerland. The first thing I learned was to limit my human interactions to a minimum level, which was quite the opposite of my mother country. There was more silence there, as the sharing of emotions wasn't common. However, it was natural in my previous laboratory in Italy to share the successes and failures of lab experiments. Sharing such things between scientific colleagues was a regular daily aspect of our life, a key mutual scientific learning moment and a psychological relief in the case of a very promising experiment's failure. In my new Swiss lab, scientific exchange was promoted and well accepted, but sharing sentiments, happiness, or frustration was considered overwhelming. It was something to avoid or be kept to oneself or just a few people. This was a critical point I learned that helped me to understand the culture of Zürich. Therefore, I was able to become more integrated into a country in which I would spend many years working and living successfully.

At a particular moment in my career, I was unexpectedly nominated to be part of an accelerated learning program. It was proposed to me that I spend two years in China. I was scared but also very excited to initiate a new work and life experience on a continent completely unknown to me. I would move from a very organized, ordered, and established work environment to one entirely new. I was the only foreigner in my department, so I learned for the first time what it was to *be* a diverse group member. The work environment progressed from one where the *guānxì* (foreigner) relationship was central to one where an equal working relationship was established. What my previous work environment may have only been quietly acknowledged was now considered a critical business moment and a reason for a team dinner. As the team leader, I had to establish a team/matrix method of working in an environment where the only way to lead was to have a place in the hierarchy. So, just being the team leader was sufficient to ensure that the entire team would do as I asked. However, I learned how to create a mutually respectful relationship in which every team member was empowered to provide their own scientific perspectives (ones that sometimes were different from mine, and vice versa).

I cultivated this sense of empowerment by building a great relationship with the team and its members, by always listening and trying to understand the new work environment, rather than making comparisons to my previous work experience in Switzerland. For example, I organized dinners where each team member, including myself, prepared our culinary specialties. We explained to the others how to make the dish and described the history behind it, and we sometimes added a few related personal anecdotes.

I learned and embraced a culture where the team works as an entity rather than as individuals. I realized that, in China, the understanding of team spirit was significantly evolved. I explained to my team the importance of receiving a scientifically justified alternative work solution from each team member. I also explained that this was considered by me not as disrespectful behavior but as an opportunity to grow scientifically, develop innovation, and together make our team more successful. All these aspects were ultimately demonstrated by our company's development of effective new technological approaches for the first time. And this was an environment in which the common—and biased—belief was that China was still unable to innovate.

Moving back to Switzerland was effectively a reverse cultural shock. The China experience was very intense and pivotal for my career and greatly impacted my work-philosophy approach and behavior regarding inclusion and diversity. For the first time in my life, I had been the only example of diversity in my work environment. In Switzerland, I had to slow down my "work watch" again. I had returned from a very fast-paced country—

in full-speed development mode—to a very established country that, in consequence, was much slower and had an individualistic way of life.

At one point, I was approached by a large Israeli company. They proposed that I work for them in Switzerland in not-for-profit programs, which is my passion and life's mission! Despite being very content at my company, I decided to accept this offer, primarily because I was very happy to gain not-for-profit-program experience and, further, to start from zero in the development of a new unit. Simultaneously, it meant working in an Israeli company culture that I did not know well but assumed would likely have a different method of working. Although, as I would later share with my new colleagues, I soon discovered that there are so many similarities with the Mediterranean culture of my heritage.

I learned to flex from an environment in which a direct and respectful conflict of opinions was avoided (being considered too direct and, potentially, too personal) to one in which directness was regarded as a normal (and "must-do") way of working toward progress (and was not considered at all personal). Many times, after a very intense and respectful difference of opinions in a meeting, I would go with my colleagues for an after-work moment together. Business was business and was separated from the pleasure of spending time with a great colleague in the informal bar or restaurant setting. This was very exciting for me, as it was very similar to my own nature—using directness as a tool to make work more effective. I also experienced how we could develop an ordered, innovative, and well-defined strategy from the *balagan* (a Hebrew term meaning "chaos"). This required a cultural shift—where I was living, chaos was considered a negative way to work—to adjust to the local norm that all work actions needed to have written rules. As such, I experienced intense emotional-intelligence experiences with some of my Israeli colleagues, the nature of which I had only experienced before with my closest family members and friends.

I recently moved to the United States to work in an organization fully dedicated to not-for-profit programs in low- and middle-income countries. Europeans tend to think that we know a lot about the USA, thanks to the multiple cultural and economic exchanges that the two continents have historically had. I decided to move away from this common assumption, to instead listen and observe once more—and, in doing so, to form an opinion as an unbiased person living for the first time on a new continent and in a new nation. It is again so exciting and an enriching experience for myself and my colleagues as we strive for very similar and aligned work values and objectives, although we achieve them in different ways sometimes. My own experiences have taught me something fundamental: listening, observing, and communicating—and having a constant, respectful mutual understanding and exchange with the people from the specific country you are in—are the key ingredients of the recipe for a successful and pleasant inclusion and diversity experience for you and your team alike.

Chapter 8

THE CULTURAL DIMENSION OF COMMUNICATION

THE WORLD COMMUNICATES IN MANY different ways, and most cultures have their own norms. Communication is essential, in person and online.

Communication is not just *what* we say—it is also *how* we say it. People become accustomed to sharing information in a certain way; thus, in addition to *what* they say, it is important *how* they say it. In many societies, how people appear and how they look at look you when they are speaking are as important as the words they use. In all cultures, nonverbal communication either enhances or detracts from the verbal message, but it is considered more carefully in some than others. It is conveyed in body language, eye contact, hand and body gestures, and even seating positions at business meetings.

Equally important is the amount of information individuals feel inclined to share. Cultures convey different amounts of information when they communicate. The amount of information is typically driven by the culture's perception of how much detail, background, and projection is necessary for the information to be "actionable" by the listener.

In cultures in which communication has a lower value, people look for content, not what surrounds the content. Low-communication cultures, like the US or Australia, are more direct and explicit in the way they communicate with one another.

In high-communication cultures, like France or India, the context of communication is *very* important. It is not what people say that is most important; it is the tone of voice and where the conversation takes place. It might be more important *how* something is said rather than *what* actually was said. People tend to be indirect. Listeners are expected to interpret statements and questions or to infer what the listener is saying. Speaking eloquently and indirectly is a valued art. The issue of saving face is always a concern in high-communication cultures. This concept refers to the honor and respect that can be given to another person by making sure your message lands on them well.

In low-communication cultures, business meetings are held to share the general and necessary information needed to accomplish a given task. In most situations, decisions are expected to be made by the end of the meeting. There is little tolerance for putting off decisions until a second meeting about the same topic.

In cultures such as Japan, face-to-face communication is preferred, especially when giving negative feedback. In these high-communication cultures, in-person meetings are preferred and expected when possible. This is in contrast to a culture such as Germany or the United States, where the efficiency of email or a phone call is often preferred.

In cultures in which communication has lower value, people will look for content, not what surrounds the range. Directness and brevity are considered assets when communicating. Too much context indicates the person's lack of ability to summarize and get to the point. Specifically, when building a slide presentation or a summary, less is better.

For example, the Scandinavian countries are very "conservative" with their use of words. They do not speak much and have concise, precise phrases or words for most required communication. Much like the US Americans, Scandinavian's are taught to provide less context and detail. Then if the other person has questions, they will ask.

Alternatively, in a high-context and high-communication culture, more is better. The belief is that by providing more context, you are making sure that the other person doesn't feel foolish by having to ask questions. Once again, it's "saving face." Specifically, when building a slide presentation, one would be expected to include more content and visuals. In addition, the tone of voice and location of the conversations are equally as important.

BEST PRACTICE FOR MANAGERS IN LOW-COMMUNICATION CULTURES

Individuals in low-communication cultures are comfortable with direct feedback. Feedback recipients in low-communication cultures tend not to think of constructive criticism as something to be taken personally and instead want to know the facts. Skip the small talk: feedback sessions do not need to involve much up-front chat. The context in which you give feedback, including nonverbal signs and behavior, plays a more significant role for the one receiving the feedback. Plan to create a positive experience using mutual respect and consideration.

- Any positive feedback given should be specific and to the point. Flamboyant language and public praise may not be well received.

- Feedback should focus on the behavior, whether positive or in need of improvement.

- Specific and objective examples of the issues and a measurable metric for ongoing performance should be provided.

- The tone of voice and nonverbal indicators are critical in low-communication cultures, so it is advisable to watch any body language and to favor in-person or video meetings.

- The right place and method of communication should be chosen in advance.

- It is appropriate to be cautious with written feedback so as not to be seen as dismissive or rude.

- Overly wordy praise and recognition should be avoided; respect and sincerity will work better.

BEST PRACTICE FOR MANAGERS IN HIGH-COMMUNICATION CULTURES

Individuals in high-communication societies need direct feedback that uses more indirect language and avoids personal criticism. Individuals in high-communication cultures are likely to be relationship oriented. Critical feedback can cause the recipient to feel as though they have failed the group they work with and, thus, feel shame.

Criticism should focus on how to assist the group in meeting its objectives rather than the recipient or personal issues. Feedback sessions in high-communication cultures should be flexible in terms of the end time, depending on the level and nature of the general conversation generated as part of the dialogue.

- Feedback should be given in person. Use video calls as a second option. Face-to-face communication is preferred and allows the giver to gauge reactions and body language.

- Regular one-on-one sessions should be used in order to create a cadence of feedback, build trust, and reduce anxiety over receiving criticism or guidance.

- Additional time for questions and a check for understanding should be planned and scheduled. Feedback should not be rushed, as it may feel dismissive. An extended discussion should be prepared, along with plentiful information. Data and metrics are essential in high-communication cultures.

- Specific tasks or actions oriented toward improvement should be the focus. It is necessary to prepare for the discussion beforehand and to plan to ask for ideas from the recipient. Positive contributions should be emphasized to the group or team so as to build esteem and offer support and coaching to meet the goals. The conversation should be a collaborative two-way discussion rather than a directive.

- Remember to "save face" by focusing on respect and treating the person with honor.

- Positive feedback should be specific and indicate outcomes. Instead of saying, "Great job," say, "I appreciate your hard work getting the project plan to all meeting attendees ahead of schedule, as it saves time for the team." People want to know the specifics of praise.

- Thank-you notes and emails with specific information are required.

KNOWING YOURSELF—COMMUNICATION

The three scenarios below relate to the cultural dimension of communication. The most natural response to each indicates where one may fall on the communication-dimension scale. There is no right or wrong answer. Individuals may find themselves in a place on the scale different than what is the cultural norm for their home country. This may be due to having lived in countries other than or experiencing other influences within their country of origin. It can also be due to having experienced a working environment different from the origin country's cultural norms.

Scenario 1

Your sales team in Japan has underperformed this year. You need to reflect on its results and provide the team members with goals for the next quarter.

Response A: You email team Japan and highlight that the most recent result is highly disappointing, asking them all (including their manager) to improve performance.

Response B: You travel to Japan and meet with the team manager in person. You discuss the fact that your company must increase earnings. You share your expectations for the next quarter.

In low-communication cultures, the efficiency of email or a phone call is an entirely acceptable means of communication. Therefore, Response A would be appropriate.

High-communication cultures are usually also high-relationship cultures, so in-person meetings or video calls are preferred and expected whenever possible. Response B would, therefore, be an appropriate strategy in such locations.

Scenario 2

You are at a conference and hope to get a chance to network with other IT specialists.

Response A: You introduce yourself to attendees and offer them your business card. You share a little about your job, your company, and why you are there.

Response B: You introduce yourself to attendees and offer them your business card. You share a little about your job and then try to create a deeper connection by asking them about anything interesting they have found to do in the city.

Low-communication cultures are "conservative" with their use of words. Short, precise phrases tend to be utilized for most required communications. Therefore, Response A would be the appropriate level of communication in such locations.

In high-communication cultures, what would be "on point" in low-communication cultures might be looked upon as too brief to inspire trust. In these situations, Response B would be the better approach.

Scenario 3

You are creating a PowerPoint presentation for a new product that you are launching.

Response A: You create a succinct presentation with only a few slides and bullets. You choose not to include lots of images and content.

Response B: You create a presentation with lots of content—words, graphs, charts, and images. You are pleased because you've given your audience a full understanding of the benefits and product differentiators.

In cultures where communication has a lower value, people will look for content, not what surrounds it. Directness and brevity are considered assets when communicating. Too much context indicates the person's lack of ability to summarize and get to the point. Specifically, when building a slide presentation, less is better. Otherwise, people will think you didn't prepare adequately and didn't take the time to analyze and organize the information. Response A would, therefore, be an appropriate response in such settings.

Alternatively, in a high-communication culture, Response B would be the right approach (as more is better). Specifically, when building a slide presentation, one would be expected to include more content and visuals. This would indicate that you had spent an appropriate amount of time preparing for the meeting.

KNOWING TEAM COLLEAGUES

Understanding the differences between the use of low and high orientations of communication in global team situations.

Team Members

Hugo (High-Communication-Orientation Colombian National)

Hugo is the sales manager for a company in Colombia. He has many years of industry experience and knows most of the leadership in Latin America on a friendly basis. Hugo understands how to get business done in Latin America, but he has been disappointed by the past lack of cultural understanding from the US-based leadership.

Adriana (Low-Communication-Orientation US American of Mexican Heritage)

Adriana has spent ten years in sales at the same company and has consistently delivered good results for the company. Three years ago, she was made regional sales manager for the Great Lakes region to reward her success. Her stellar performance in that role has earned her a big recent promotion to sales manager for the Americas. Adriana is excited about the new position, as she loves what she does and has always wanted to work internationally. She now has a team of regional sales managers based in Canada, the United States, and Latin America.

COMMUNICATION

LOW   - - -   - -   -   +   + +   + + +   HIGH

Adriana   Hugo

Scenario

Adriana is responsible for the Americas regions: the US, Canada, and Latin America. She has seven managers and wants to start her new role successfully by meeting with them individually. She needs to review the performance of each regional manager to set expectations and goals for the coming year. Adriana will report her findings and recommendations to the C-suite, and she has little time to gather information since the year-end is in a few weeks.

She decides to approach each of the upcoming discussions differently, taking culture into account. She will need to ask many questions in these meetings and give feedback on current performance.

What actions could Adriana take to keep the communication dimension in mind?

1. Review her own cultural profile for communication.

   Adriana is proud of her Mexican heritage, although she has never lived in Mexico. When reviewing the results of her cultural profile, she tracked primarily as a US American in the communication dimension.

   Mexican Americans like Adriana may have cultural preferences opposite those of a Mexican national working in the United States.

2. Consider the cultural profiles.

   When Adriana considers the cultural profiles of the countries in which she is working, she will learn which of her team members are in high-communication societies and which are in low-communication ones. Adriana realizes there are cultural differences within her region—specifically a disparity between North, Central, and South America—and takes this into account when making her plans. She decides to meet with the Latin American managers since they value personal relationships and are less direct. For the US and Canada, she decides that video calls would suffice. Communication preferences for these two countries are low, meaning that meetings and feedback can be more concise and straightforward.

   Even within a given country, there will likely be communication differences. For example, Adriana allows extra time for calls with managers in the southern US states because she understands that they value a more extended and interactive discussion in that region of the US.

Even though a region may seem homogenous, variances in how people communicate are essential to recognize. Be careful to review each one and consider them individually. Then, Adriana will have better insight into the best ways to communicate with them and will understand what does not work after she builds trust with the managers in each country.

3. Consider communication preferences.

Adriana schedules one-on-one, in-person meetings with the regional managers in Latin America. She ensures that her travel itinerary enables her to have a full day available to spend with them in their location. Adriana schedules the meetings early, thus keeping the rest of the day free in case any extra time is needed.

Latin Americans are typically higher in the relationship dimension and will appreciate the extra time spent talking in person. This more relational communication style means that one should allow more time to speak and not rush the conversation. Scheduling more time will enable Adriana to build trust by extending discussions as needed.

4. Align with communication preferences.

Adriana reviews the preferences of the Latin American countries she is working with and sees that people in high-communication cultures are likely to be relationship oriented. She does her homework on each Latin American regional manager's background and provides feedback during the meetings conversationally and collaboratively. Adriana outlines the team goals for the year ahead for each Latin American region and makes sure everyone is clear on the plans.

Because Latin Americans score high on communication preferences, she will focus on group goals and each person's role with those goals is more effective than focusing on individual goals.

5. Focus feedback on behaviors and tasks, not the person.

Adriana makes sure that she has specific and objective examples of issues for each person, particularly regarding areas of improvement. She avoids personal criticism, particularly in Latin America, where the preference is for providing alternative methods to meet goals. Adriana uses metrics and data to support desired outcomes and acknowledges what team members are doing well in all the feedback discussions with managers.

High-communication cultures may feel offended or embarrassed to be called out individually for failures such as not meeting goals because they communicate more implicitly than explicitly. Giving feedback that acknowledges positive efforts along with areas of improvement builds trust.

6. Take the culture into account.

Company policy states that all business meetings and communications must be in English. However, Adriana speaks adequate Spanish and uses the language to help her bond with Latin American managers outside of official discussions and during lunch. The day after her visit, Adriana sends each of the regional managers an email summarizing their discussion and outlining the goals for the year ahead. She includes a personal comment, such as one expressing how much she enjoyed meeting them during her visit, and she thanks them for their time spent together the previous day.

Following up with the entire team is a good idea but making an effort to personalize the email will be appreciated by high-communication individuals. Summarizing the overall group goals keeps the focus on the group. Using more indirect language and avoiding personal criticism are best practices for giving feedback in this group.

7. Flex your style.

Adriana's trip to Latin America uses up quite a lot of time, so she conducts her discussions with the North American regional managers via videoconference. She spends less time with this group because this approach aligns with these individuals' communication preferences. Understanding this helps her to be more effective as a leader.

Adriana prepares specific and objective examples of the issues while giving measurable metrics for each manager's performance in the year ahead. Following the video call, she sends a follow-up email outlining the discussion.

One of the most significant errors global managers make is treating all discussions, particularly feedback and performance reviews, in the same way. Adapting the method of communication (video call versus face-to-face) and focus of the conversation (individual versus group) allows Adriana to connect better with each group.

KNOWING WHERE

The dimension of communication around the world:

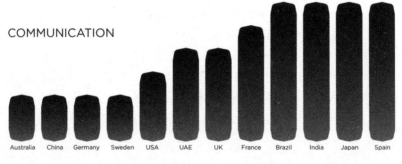

COMMUNICATION

Australia China Germany Sweden USA UAE UK France Brazil India Japan Spain

LOW   **HIGH**

Low-Communication Culture

A country with one of the lowest-communication cultures in the world is Sweden.

Some Cultural Etiquette Observations for Swedish Business Settings

In Sweden, the common form of greeting is a firm handshake for both men and women. When addressing business counterparts, one should initially follow the traditional practice of using titles and last names, although Swedes will usually move quickly onto first-name terms. Punctuality is the more critical element of doing business in Sweden, and any delays in arriving at a meeting should be advised ahead of time whenever possible. This propensity toward punctuality extends to the business meeting itself, and as such very little "small talk" is required prior to the official dialogue. Another notable characteristic of Swedish business life is equality within company structures. This can lead to a more-junior employee being charged with the final negotiation of a business agreement once it has been approved by the leaders of the enterprise. Sweden has one of the world's highest levels of gender equality, so business visitors should watch for any gender-based unconscious bias.

High-Communication Culture

A country with one of the highest-communication cultures in the world is Thailand.

Some Cultural Etiquette Observations for Thai Business Settings

Business relationships develop slowly in Thailand, as Thais will want to get to know you well, so it can take many meetings over months, or even years, to forge a successful partnership—a one-off visit or mere habit of videoconferencing will not usually be sufficient. It is difficult for most Thais to criticize or give a direct yes/no response to a certain question. It is best—whenever possible—to avoid putting a Thai business partner in an awkward position.

If possible, business cards should be printed in Thai on one side and offered faceup with both hands. The person with the highest social status receives the business card first. Cards should similarly be received with both hands and should be studied before putting away. A polite comment is always appreciated. It is inappropriate to write on a card or put it in a back pocket in front of the person who has just supplied it. Any business presentation should be factual and easy to understand, with facts and figures included to back up any conclusions. High-pressure sales tactics should be avoided.

As Thailand is a hierarchical society, issues may need extensive discussion at all levels (often over lunch or dinner) before final decisions are made by senior management. Indeed, the purpose of talks in such settings is less about business and more about relationships. The Thai host will almost certainly pay for the meal. It is not appropriate for a visitor to insist on paying.

Thais most typically greet each other with the *wai*, whereby the hands are raised with the fingers pointing upward, as if in prayer, and the head is slightly bowed. The junior person does so first, and the senior person then responds. However, westerners are usually not expected to know the hierarchical etiquette regarding how much to bow the head. Most Thai businesses will likely offer a handshake to foreign visitors, but the *wai* will always be appreciated.

VIGNETTE: OBSERVATIONS OF AN AMERICAN IN THAILAND...AND OTHER ADVENTURES

By Christine Sperr, Managing Director, Santa Fe Relocation

I spent the first thirty years of my life living within a fifty-kilometer radius of where I was born. That is different from saying that I didn't travel. Each summer we loaded up the Dodge Charger with my grandparents and made it our mission to check off a visit to each state within the continental US. Also, in college, I was privileged to win a partial scholarship for the "Semester at Sea" program and travel around the world with 740 other students on a repurposed OOCL vessel, which was fully kitted out with classrooms, a library, and the essential pub. But it wasn't until I was working in relocation services that I felt the intense longing to move overseas.

After completing a successful implementation program in Asia for a leading Fast Moving Consumer Goods company (FMCG), I began a wonderful and truly global adventure. I packed up all my belongings and relocated to Bangkok. I loved the heightened state of sensory overload—the sights, sounds, smells, and tastes of Thailand were so vastly different from Colorado. Culturally, it could not have been more different from working in the US, as I had to learn the delicate art of kind persuasion, master tactfully handling passive-aggressive behavior, and, above all, create a work environment full of *sanuk*, or "fun."

After focusing on *sanuk* and supporting the market entry of two major automotive giants into Thailand, I received a call asking if I would interview for a role in the Middle East. My first thought was: "Why in the world would they want a single, white, US-American female for the Middle East?" I was intrigued! After a marathon interview with a panel of middle-aged Indian men and a thorough review of my birth time and date, in which my celestial chart revealed that I would be an auspicious fit, I packed my suitcase and ventured to Dubai. Honestly, I didn't know what to expect, as I had hardly had any exposure to Arab culture and could barely pinpoint the United Arab Emirates on the map. My introduction to the country was filled with humorous anecdotes and, at times, frustrating and lonely nights, but in the end, it was my friends and colleagues who won my heart. In the UAE, only 10 percent to 11 percent of the population is indigenous, so I was lucky to work with a diverse cast of international colleagues who helped build and grow the company as well as help me mature as a manager.

In the Middle East, I had to develop my persuasion skills further and focus on slowing down and getting to know people and clients before jumping right into a business-focused conversation. It would be extremely impolite if I didn't ask about how one's family was doing or how they spent the summer. Launching directly into a business discussion would end in disaster. This would not be evident during the meeting; however, you would never progress to working together if you did not invest in first building rapport. Also, I had to know when to become aggressive and draw a hard line in the sand. In Thailand, you never acted outwardly aggressively. This is why there is such a prevalence of passive aggressiveness. However, in the Middle East, it was often suitable and even required to raise your voice and passionately express your position. Lastly, I quickly learned that shaking a man's hand or nonchalantly touching someone could be deemed culturally inappropriate, so I had to dial down my casual familiarity several octaves.

Although I loved Dubai, another opportunity beckoned, and I relocated to Switzerland for a five-year stint working in seaports throughout southern Italy. Talk about taking a full 180-degree culture shift! Not only were Switzerland and the UAE vastly different but working in both Italy and Switzerland provided an entire case study on the differences between two countries so close in proximity but so distant in mentality. Although this professional role brought with it an abundance of incredible experiences, the draw to return to the Middle East was overpowering. My passion for global mobility, love of sunshine, and desire to be back among the sand and sea boomeranged me back to Dubai. Upon returning, I discovered new buildings, unfamiliar neighborhoods, and a much more progressive business setting. Culturally, "old" Dubai still lingered, but a woman could wear slightly more revealing clothing (as in showing an upper arm or knee). I also found that the "timeliness" standard of meetings had changed to more closely resemble my Swiss clock and not my Middle Eastern clock, as chronic tardiness became less frequent and even government offices opened punctually at the stated time. But, in the end, people are people all over the world, and the success of assimilation comes through mutual understanding, tolerance, and respect.

IT'S ABOUT TIME!

Christine's journey has caused her to experience countries that vary widely in terms of a number of the cultural dimensions outlined in previous chapters. One example is as it relates to time.

In moving from her native United States to Thailand, Christine transitioned from a country at the highest end of the time-dimension scale to one at the lowest level. In then moving on to Dubai, Christine arrived in a country higher on the time-dimension scale than the one she left, although still far from the time-dimension norm of the United States. In subsequently moving to Switzerland, Christine once more experienced the highest end of the time-dimension scale (as Switzerland tracks similarly to the United States on this dimension scale).

Chapter 9

THE CULTURAL DIMENSION OF HIERARCHY

KNOWING OTHERS

Hierarchy reflects many of a society's fundamental values—that is, how does an organization see rank, and how does it demonstrate the relative value of its members?

In cultures such as Sweden, the Netherlands, and the US, there is little importance placed on hierarchy. In fact, it is believed that anybody can grow up to be the president of a multimillion-dollar business, and it's common for people to use first names.

However, in most of Asia, it is believed that people should "know their place" by accepting their rank. In these hierarchical cultures, people are even addressed according to their status by a series of titles and honorifics. Even neighbors will refer to each other by a title and never assume that they may call someone by a first name, no matter how long they have known the acquaintance. These cultures' languages have several words for "you," each of which indicates a different level of familiarity. Status symbols such as cars, expensive clothes, and jewelry sometimes provide important clues to a person's societal rank.

In high-hierarchy cultures, managers are expected to be decision-makers. They often watch over all aspects of their subordinates. Most leaders from less hierarchical cultures, like the US and the Netherlands, will struggle when they work in or lead teams in more hierarchical cultures like Latin America or Spain, and France. Feedback on the leaders often describes them as being weak and indecisive and someone who can't make decisions on their own. When I consult with executives and CEOs from Fortune 500 companies who struggle to maximize performance in those cultures, I find that those leaders haven't recognized that hierarchical cultures lead and manage differently. Meaning the US style of leadership is very facilitative while hierarchical cultures expect leaders to be more directive. Of course, those same leaders will tell me that they can't work that way and that they need collaboration. By flexing, you can get your teams in those countries to meet you in the middle between facilitative and directive and that is called the inventive space. You have to first begin by giving them permission to do something they've never been allowed or even expected to do, because it would seem as though they were overstepping their position. Many executives seem surprised by this, so I have to explain to them that educational systems in other countries teach very differently and organizations in those countries define leadership differently. The US, Scandinavia, and a handful of other countries are actually the anomalies in terms of our facilitative management style. Most cultures around the world lead with a more directive style. Therefore, you have to have a very frank conversation about how you want them to show up in your meetings and your expectations around their contributions, thought leadership, and debate.

Be aware that there are many cultures that (intentionally) do not teach critical thinking or critical reasoning within their educational systems.

Low-hierarchy cultures typically see managers as facilitators—leaders who help employees do their best work, not simply those who make decisions. Good managers empower employees and expect them to take responsibility and believe in empowerment and in the right of everyone to be heard. At work, everyone can move up the organizational ranks based on performance.

Leaders and associates exhibiting the characteristics of low-hierarchy cultures should expect resistance from those raised in a more hierarchical environment because those cultures will be more concerned about the chain of command than efficiency.

BEST PRACTICE FOR MANAGERS IN LOW-HIERARCHY CULTURES

In low-hierarchy more egalitarian cultures, feedback is more of a discussion than a directive activity. Let the recipient speak up and share their opinions and ideas regarding the discussed issues. While a subordinate will show respect for their boss, the leader should be prepared to facilitate a dialogue where the participants are on an equal footing—one, therefore, more informal than that of a highly hierarchical society. Both parties should plan and outline the required level of performance following a feedback session and agree upon the expectations.

In a low-hierarchy culture, an employee's self-perceived level of responsibility in the organization is high. They view all opinions and ideas as valid and expect a place at the table, regardless of title. Low-hierarchy cultures require ongoing flexibility, as leaders frequently hear new ideas from all levels of an organization. Brainstorming ideas for improvement and collaboration are common ways of problem-solving. Employees expect to participate in problem-solving and provide advice and direction to leaders. Constructive feedback may evolve into a lengthy discussion.

- Both peers and leaders can provide input; engage in group feedback through brainstorming and collaboration sessions to solve problems.

- Developmental feedback should be prepared in advance and include concrete areas of improvement; it is appropriate to focus on the behavior or task at hand and keep feedback to the individual rather than to the group.

- Be prepared to shut down long discussions or arguments about the feedback you are giving. Ask for ideas, then create a path and outline follow-up actions.

- Defensive debates or discussions should be avoided when developmental feedback is not well received. Instead, restate the steps needed for improvement.

- Coaching through regular and informal feedback can be successful with this cultural dimension.

BEST PRACTICE FOR MANAGERS IN HIGH-HIERARCHY CULTURES

In a high-hierarchy culture, those in senior positions and those with higher tenure are automatically more respected. These cultures view senior figures as responsible for directing a company's success rather than subject to critique and input from across all levels of the organization. Decisions are made at the top and accepted by the employees. The primary measure of employee success is that of doing as instructed and doing it well.

Feedback should be given by the manager or a more-senior person, not by peers. Be specific about areas of improvement—those that still need to meet expectations. The recipient is likely to be deferential in such situations and may not ask many questions or challenge the feedback. This response doesn't demonstrate a lack of assertiveness or interest. Senior figures should be measured in their comments, as their subordinates are likely to take the feedback literally. Employees expect leaders to solve problems and give them direction.

- Positive feedback will be well accepted and can be given in a group.

- Employees expect to hear from the leader—rather than from their peers—regarding performance issues. The leader should deliver feedback and should not pass on the burden to others. The most-senior person involved should provide the feedback.

- Be specific and check for understanding when giving developmental feedback.

- The recipient should know that they are valued and are doing well.

- Good ideas can often go unspoken in a high-hierarchy culture, so they should be specifically requested.

- Specific steps for improvement should be provided when giving developmental feedback.

- The task or behavior should be the focus, not personal attributes.

KNOWING YOURSELF—HIERARCHY

The two scenarios below relate to the cultural dimension of hierarchy. The most natural response to each indicates where one may fall on the hierarchy-dimension scale. There is no right or wrong answer. Individuals may find themselves different than what is the cultural norm for their home country. This may be due to having lived in other countries, or may also be due to having experienced a working environment different from the cultural norms of the origin country.

Scenario 1

> Your manager is out sick today. You are the next-level manager even though you've been on the team for just a few days.
>
> **Response A:** There is someone with more experience on the team. You feel more comfortable letting them lead the morning briefing, as you've **been with the company for only a short time.**
>
> **Response B:** As the next-level manager in charge, even with limited knowledge, you take over the morning briefing.

High-hierarchy cultures expect that leaders are decisive and follow the chain of command. They do not view power as achievable by everyone. In such locations, Response B would be a good idea.

In low-hierarchy cultures, Response A would be entirely appropriate and seen as being collaborative and egalitarian.

Scenario 2

Your manager lets you conduct most of the research and financial planning for his projects. During your manager's lunch break, you answer his phone. It is your CEO, who has a question regarding a current project.

Response A: You know the answer to the question. You explain that you are an assistant and offer the answer to the CEO. You ask your manager to call the CEO after his meeting.

Response B: You tell the CEO that your manager will call him back as soon as he returns from his lunch break. You prepare the required research for your manager and remind your manager to call the CEO.

Individuals raised solely in a low-hierarchy culture are likely to gravitate to Response A. Such cultures believe that power is distributed evenly. Therefore, everybody with knowledge can and should speak up to keep the company running as efficiently as possible.

Individuals raised solely in high-hierarchy cultures are likely to prioritize the given hierarchy of an organization over its efficiency. In this situation, Response B would be appropriate. The individual involved could otherwise be seen as overstepping their manager or as disrespectful to the CEO.

KNOWING TEAM COLLEAGUES

It is understanding the differences between the low and high orientation of time in global team situations.

Team Members

Greg (Low-Hierarchy-Orientation French American Dual National)

Greg was born in France to French parents. When Greg was the age of five, his father relocated to New Jersey for a job. The whole family has remained in the United States ever since. Greg went to university in Connecticut, majoring in marketing and communications. Since then, he has worked in Pennsylvania with the marketing team at the US headquarters of DuBois Chemie. Having introduced several new marketing initiatives, Greg is considered a rising star. The organization has introduced a program for employees to work in other global locations. Due to Greg's French heritage and fluency, he has secured a job at the headquarters on the edge of Paris. Greg has now been in France for three months. He was very excited about both the promotion and the opportunity to live in the country of his birth. Yet, now, he is struggling to settle into office life.

HIERARCHY

LOW — – – | – – | – | + | + + | + + + — HIGH

                     Greg   **Maria**

Scenario

Despite holding a position superior to the one he held in the US, Greg already feels less autonomous than he did previously. He understood that the company wanted to hear about new ideas so as to utilize the best in every aspect of the enterprise. Greg has been disappointed that his valuable marketing experience in the US counts for nothing in France.

Greg's boss, Gilles, has a set way of doing things and does not seem open to Greg's feedback on potential improvements. Greg thinks this is partly due to the lesser amount of ongoing interaction between team members. He is also finding that his fluency in French is a disadvantage, as it causes his boss and colleagues to forget that he is from somewhere else. Ultimately, Greg feels alone.

Greg wants this assignment to succeed despite his misgivings. He feels that his boss is unapproachable regarding personal matters, so Greg discusses his problems with the HR department. His company reminds him that they have a digital cultural-coaching solution, and they advise him to complete his cultural assessment.

What should Greg do to be successful?

1. Look at his cultural profile regarding hierarchy.

   In completing his own personal profile, Greg finds that he is at the end of the hierarchy spectrum opposite to that of France (which is indeed at the highest point on the scale). Greg then understands more clearly that the actions of his boss—and his colleagues—should not be taken too personally. Greg needs to understand his cultural profile in order to learn where to flex to achieve better business outcomes.

2. Consider the culture.

   Greg needs to understand the work culture of France and his French colleagues. He decides to learn more about the culture, particularly the hierarchy dimension, so that he can give and receive feedback more effectively.

   Understanding cultural preferences will allow him to flex his approach to be more effective when working with his boss and colleagues. In discussions, he will give feedback in a more readily accepted way. He may also begin to break down some barriers and develop a more comfortable working relationship with his team by applying what he learns.

3. Be prepared to flex his style.

   Greg was born in France and is fluent in the language. However, he lived and studied for much of his life in the US, meaning that his cultural preferences are likely quite different from those of his French peers. The way he previously learned to give and receive feedback could be achieved better in this new job, and Greg now realizes that the hierarchical nature of a company in France causes the giving of upward feedback to be an unfamiliar event. He decides to save his ideas for discussion in the regular team meetings with the team's manager. Greg concludes that a longer-term view is required and that his boss will only be able or willing to process some of his ideas at a time. He now starts to deliver his feedback in stages.

4. Get outside help or coaching when needed.

Greg reaches out to some peers and asks for their advice on working with the team. By requesting feedback, he establishes a more open relationship. He listens to their advice and seeks clarification when needed.

KNOWING WHERE

The dimension of hierarchy around the world:

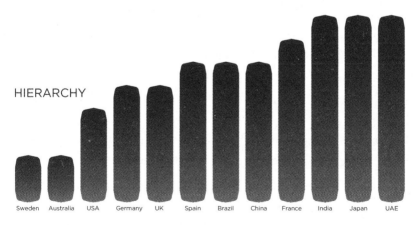

HIERARCHY

Sweden Australia USA Germany UK Spain Brazil China France India Japan UAE

LOW   HIGH

High-Hierarchy Culture

A country with one of the highest-hierarchy cultures in the world is Panama.

Some Cultural Etiquette Observations for Panamanian Business Settings

Punctuality is respected and followed in Panamanian business circles, especially for overseas counterparts. It is advisable to have a clear understanding of whether an event is a business meeting or strictly a social gathering. This is important because business meetings often occur in a restaurant setting.

The customary greeting in Panama is a firm handshake with direct eye contact. Women customarily make the first move when it comes to shaking another's hand. Men do not assume that women are willing to greet them, so they may wait for a female counterpart to take the lead.

In business meetings, it is appropriate to first allow enough time to chat about matters unrelated to the business context. The rushing of this exchange could be considered disrespectful. One should remember to address others using titles and their last name until invited to do otherwise.

As in most Latin American countries, it is not wise to criticize or pull rank on the other person in Panama. One should also expect Latin Americans to communicate within a close personal space. Expectations regarding body space between individuals are much different from, for instance, those of North America.

High-Hierarchy Culture

A country with one of the highest-hierarchy cultures in the world is France.

Some Cultural Etiquette Observations for French Business Settings

In France, a firm handshake is the standard form of greeting in business settings. Men should always wait for a woman to extend her hand before offering a handshake. The rich culture of France requires attention to detail when addressing others. The formal custom is to rise when being introduced to someone. When addressing others by name, one should always use title and last name, and *Madame* is used to address both women and young girls. Children and the younger generation are more apt to use first names.

The business visitor is not usually expected or required to speak French. For those that do, it is imperative to use the formal *vous* form of communicating until a French counterpart advises that the time has come to switch to the informal *tu* form. In business settings, titles (*Mr.*, *Mrs.*, or the professional term) should be used with the surname. In other words, politeness is valued more highly in France than in many other European countries.

Punctuality is a sign of politeness in France, so it is necessary to arrive at the agreed-upon time. Business cards should be printed in French on one side. Given the French love of debating, business decisions may take longer than in other countries. Business lunches and dinners also take longer in France than elsewhere, although personal matters are usually discussed at a shorter length.

VIGNETTE: HIERARCHY AT ITS FINEST

By Ismael Kossih, Luxury Brands
Digital Marketing, Dubai

Born and raised in Brussels, Belgium, I am of mixed heritage, as my parents are Belgian and Moroccan. As such, I was taught from a young age that we are all unique. Since childhood, I've been surrounded by three different languages: Arabic, French, and Flemish. I am lucky to have grown up in a cosmopolitan city such as Brussels.

Through my master's degree in digital communication, I learned that most luxury brands nowadays focus on their ethics to attract a new generation of customers, one that is conscientious about ESG.

I worked for a luxury fashion brand in London, where I experienced respect and social equality, where managers were seen as coaches. In contrast, I then moved to Dubai where people were just pushed and told to make numbers at any price. The management style in Dubai was not at all collaborative. Perhaps that was just my impression, as I didn't understand the codes. The message, however, seemed to be to make money and sell at any cost including your health! Ironically, the brand I was working for sold itself, as it was the most timelessly desired French luxury brand in the world (the name spoke for itself). In other words, it wasn't necessary to treat employees the way they were treated.

Instead of developing resentment upon finding myself experiencing this style of management, I wanted to figure out why it was like this. I understood that it was not personal and that the rest of my colleagues weren't happy in this culture or environment either. I realized in talking to them that this management style was rooted in an extremely hierarchical culture. One where you are always directed or told exactly what to do. It was the exact opposite of the more collaborative culture that I was accustomed to in my previous roles.

By understanding this, I could better cope or flex with the environment from a professional and personal standpoint. For me, traveling and meeting people from other cultures feeds the soul. There will be no end to my quest for knowledge about other cultures until I've visited the rest of this beautiful Earth!

DECIPHERING THE CODES

Ismael uses a very apt phrase when he says, "I didn't understand the codes." Deciphering "the codes" makes for an appropriate euphemism for describing a head-on encounter with a different cultural environment. He transitioned from the culture of his birthplace, Belgium, to that of the United Arab Emirates via the United Kingdom. In doing so, Ismael journeyed from cultures located at the center of the hierarchy-dimension scale to one on the high end. This in part explains the differences in management style that he encountered along the way. Similarly, Belgium is at the lowest end of the change-tolerance-dimension scale, while the UAE is several steps closer to the high end of the scale. This difference provided another reason why Ismael experienced such a cultural shift in his daily work environment.

Chapter 10

THE CULTURAL DIMENSION OF STATUS ATTAINMENT

IN MANY CULTURES, IT IS common to trust the individual's ability to rise above class through hard work and education. Other cultures expect you to stay in the field of your family's income level. Your family will have your back.

The dimension of status attainment refers to the importance placed on personal achievement compared to family position or other relationships in defining oneself or someone else. Beliefs regarding status attainment can also impact the hours people work, their willingness—or lack thereof—to have organizations interfere in their private lives, and the way they present themselves to others. In business interviews, status attainment impacts how interviewees present themselves, their past experiences, and their personal accomplishments.

In high-status-attainment environments like the US, accomplishments define your importance and status. Hard work and personal achievement lead to a sense of well-being. These societies are more transactional, and people are valued for their measurable contributions, hence the saying, "People live to work." Since achievements are the responsibility of individuals, those who do not make it are often looked down upon. The business encourages individual creativity and rewards hard work.

In low-status-attainment cultures, connections are more important than anything else. Status is thus related to the individuals you know and the status you had at birth, and you can hardly be blamed for not being born into the best family or having the best connections. Typically, hierarchies are clearly defined and rigid.

Those who thrive in high-status-attainment cultures like Germany or the US may feel perplexed at the amount of focus there is on family and work-life balance in low-status-attainment cultures like Spain where it isn't the norm for them to sacrifice family time on the weekends or to continuously work long days or go protracted periods of time without taking time off.

BEST PRACTICE FOR MANAGERS IN LOW-STATUS-ATTAINMENT CULTURES

Cultures with a low-status-attainment index does not mean that the individual works less than someone in a high-status-attainment society, but rather they are motivated differently. Do not assume that they lack ambition or aspiration. It simply means they have a different way of measuring their own success, and it may be less about deadlines and more about the quality of the work and cultivating strong relationships rather than just getting the job done quickly.

It is necessary to be careful when giving feedback in low-status-attainment cultures. Any relationships that the recipient may have in other parts of the enterprise may also be in play. You can still be direct, but you should exercise diplomacy and soften the edges as needed.

- Feedback should be carefully constructed. It should reflect the fact that relationships and connections are more critical than the achievement of tangible success and the symbols of achievement.

- Introductions and inclusion in meetings with well-respected people in the organization may be better than repeated positive, individual feedback.

- Developmental feedback should target expectations and what needs to happen to meet goals. Keep comments to the behavior only.

- The person may be only willing to do the minimum, so be clear on the minimum expectations. If some global expectations and norms differ from local practices, clarify them and explain the reasoning.

BEST PRACTICE FOR MANAGERS IN HIGH-STATUS-ATTAINMENT CULTURES

Cultures with a high-status index see personal achievement as primarily attained due to hard work. In a meritocracy such as this, the relationships an individual may or may not have in society do not dictate the level of attainment. Hard work and symbols of success are valued. Certifications, diplomas, college degrees, and visual signs of success are essential in this culture, as is public recognition.

When giving feedback in such cultures, the individual's contribution is paramount in framing the dialogue. The reward expected among recipients in high-status-attainment cultures is variable, as are the effort and work put in by each person to achieve the enterprise's objectives. Specific future goals should be correlated with individual efforts and explained during the discussion. Employees will want to know their projected career path in the organization. Providing ongoing coaching and feedback will help create trust, build esteem, and adjust expectations and goals as the person progresses. Expect some pushback in feedback discussions.

- Positive feedback and recognition are often public but understanding individual employee preferences are still necessary.

- High-status employees appreciate positive feedback and expect to hear when they are doing well, even if that is part of their job. Incorporate positive feedback into regular one-on-one discussions.

- Recognition programs and certificates of achievement work well in high-status cultures.

- Developmental feedback should focus on what needs to be done or changed to meet expectations.

- Performance expectations need to be very clear. High-status people want to know the metrics used to measure performance and what they need to do differently.

KNOWING YOURSELF—STATUS ATTAINMENT

The two scenarios below relate to the cultural dimension of status attainment. The most natural response to each indicates where one may fall on the status-attainment-dimension scale. There is no right or wrong answer.

Scenario 1

You are interviewing a manager for a newly created PR role.

Response A: You want to focus on those candidates who you know have built successful relationships within your organization.

Response B: You choose to focus on interviewing only the candidates with the most credentials within this field.

Low-status-attainment cultures tend to focus on people skills and other connections when making hiring decisions (Response A).

High-status-attainment cultures place most of the emphasis on an individual's ability and skills to make hiring decisions (Response B).

Scenario 2

You received an entry-level position at a large company.

Response A: You are thankful that you landed the job. The health benefits are good, and the job is a predictable nine-to-five commitment—perfect for your lifestyle.

Response B: You are determined to work hard and make your way up the organizational ladder.

You arrive early and stay late every day and often work extra on weekends. You volunteer for extra projects to build experience and make your name known in the organization.

Response A is considered generally more typical of low-status-attainment cultures. Response B is regarded as generally more typical of high-status-attainment cultures. However, this dimension—whatever the location—may feature individuals at various points on the status-attainment scale, depending on their personal and professional circumstances.

KNOWING TEAM COLLEAGUES

Understanding the low and high orientation of status attainment in global team situations.

Team Members

Hamad (Low-Status-Attainment-Orientation Qatari National)

Hamad studied in Qatar and received an opportunity to spend a semester at Texas A&M University as part of his chemical engineering program. He enjoyed the culture and maintained friendships with the people he met in Texas. His professional career has taken place with Silver Sands, where he has risen to senior manager. Hamad has made many business trips overseas in his fifteen-year career with the company. He had a temporary assignment at the Dubai office a few years ago but has otherwise always worked out of the company headquarters in Doha.

Melissa (High-Status-Attainment-Orientation American National)

Melissa is from New York and is straightforward. She rose very quickly in her previous company and was considered a high performer. Silver Sands hired her about a year ago, and Melissa would like to be the first woman promoted to senior leadership and to support other women. She recently started a Women in Leadership employee resource group (ERG), which received much attention. Melissa is one of Hamad's direct reports and the first female working at that level of the organization who he has managed.

STATUS ATTAINMENT

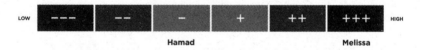

Scenario

In the short time that Melissa has spent with the company, Hamad has received many negative comments about her from colleagues at the same level (all of whom are Qatari nationals). Aside from her loud voice, her colleagues are offended that Melissa does not interact with them beyond discussing necessary work topics. In addition, they are annoyed that each day she gets to the office earlier—and stays later—than everyone else. The prevailing feeling among her colleagues is that Melissa is trying to make them look bad. Some unfavorable observations about Melissa have already bypassed Hamad and reached the C-suite. As a result, Hamad has been asked by his boss to "calm the waters."

How can Hamad best handle this situation?

1. Look at his own cultural dimensions regarding status attainment.

   Hamad is aware that the primary issue involved here is culture. In reviewing his profile's own status-attainment dimension, he can see that he rates much lower on the spectrum than Melissa, who is at the highest end of the scale.

2. Consider the national cultural dimensions of the team, determining high and low tendencies.

   As a first step toward offsetting any ongoing conflict in the office, Hamad asks that all his direct reports— including Melissa—complete their cultural profile. He instructs everyone to review their team's cultural profile to understand how these differences affect the team. Hamad hopes the exercise will increase everyone's awareness of the cultural differences between the two nationalities, particularly those on the status-attainment spectrum. Hamad then reviews the team profile.

3. Help Melissa navigate the culture.

Melissa is the anomaly among the members of Hamad's team. He, therefore, arranges a specific feedback session with her soon after the deadline for the completed profiles. Hamad does not want Melissa's personal motivation to be diminished, but he now feels that he can directly request that she make a conscious effort to flex her style to work better with the rest of the team.

Understanding the differences in the status-attainment dimension will make it easier to provide feedback on how the team perceives her. Hamad should focus on how Melissa can be more effective on his team and understand the Qatari style of working so that she can flex her style. He needs to use specific examples, such as those of her arriving first and leaving the office last, that may be seen as very positive attributes in the US but as threatening or a source of irritation in low-status-attainment cultures.

As the manager, Hamad needs to help Melissa see both sides of this dimension and provide feedback on how her behavior undermines her ability to build relationships within the organization. Understanding cultural preferences will allow him to flex his approach to be more effective when working with Melissa. In discussions, he will be able to give more readily accepted feedback that will enable her to see the negative impact her cultural reactions are having.

4. Coach the team to be more aware of cultural dimensions. Hamad should schedule a meeting so that the entire team can discuss the different dimensions, ensuring that the team understands the need to value all voices at the table. He should conduct a cultural debrief using the team profile.

KNOWING WHERE

The dimension of status attainment around the world:

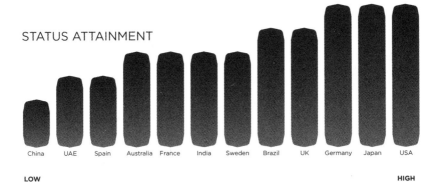

STATUS ATTAINMENT

China   UAE   Spain   Australia France   India   Sweden   Brazil   UK   Germany   Japan   USA

LOW   HIGH

Low-Status-Attainment Culture

A country with one of the lowest-status-attainment cultures in the world is Portugal.

Some Cultural Etiquette Observations for Portuguese Business Settings

The usual greeting in Portugal includes a warm handshake and direct eye contact. Men will typically wait for a woman to extend her hand before initiating the greeting. When addressing others, one should use titles and last names until invited to do otherwise. Many business meetings are held in a restaurant setting, and the business visitor should take the lead from their Portuguese host regarding the nature of the conversation (be it personal or business-oriented) at any given time.

Punctuality is required of foreigners when meeting for business. At the same time, any Portuguese counterparts that may be involved will be held to a different standard and may well arrive late. Therefore, there may be a wait time of up to twenty minutes before the meeting starts. Business meetings in Portugal require a focus on the relationship as well as on the matter at hand. A Portuguese businessperson needs to trust their overseas counterpart(s) when entering into a business deal with them.

High-Status-Attainment Culture

A country with one of the highest-status-attainment cultures in the world is Germany.

Some Cultural Etiquette Observations for German Business Settings

It is very important to be punctual in business settings in Germany. Most Germans arrive five to ten minutes early. Arriving late for a meeting is considered rude and disrespectful, and it is courteous to call ahead if one is running late. In Germany, one should expect a firm handshake when greeting both men and women. The same practice is expected when bidding farewell. Business visitors should address others by title and last name until invited to do otherwise. Business meetings in Germany are usually straight to the point and so will typically lack any lengthy introductory conversation time. Compromise, honesty, and mutual agreement are important factors to consider when doing business in Germany.

Chapter 11

THE CULTURAL DIMENSION OF GROUP ORIENTATION

KNOWING OTHERS

A culture's attitude toward group dependence is pervasive in social and business situations. These values typically take root in early childhood. Young children will be recognized either for individual accomplishments or not disturbing group harmony.

In a culture like Australia that places low importance on group orientation, business meetings are typically scheduled to maximize time, and a decision is expected by the conclusion. I often see US leaders struggling to manage or lead an organization in Australia because they don't like to be heavily managed. They are quite independent and not accustomed to being micromanaged, so there isn't the need for everyone to be part of every discussion as you so often see in the US where meetings will rarely complete all of the agenda items for a meeting because everyone is expected to give their input or their opinion. US Americans are on the highest end of the dimension while Australians are on the lowest end.

High-group-orientation cultures expect meetings to take a considerable amount of time. It is essential to allow people to voice concerns. People will resent being forced to a schedule. The goal of the meeting is typically to create a forum where everyone can voice their opinion in order for that team to be successful. Everyone must be heard, and this will prolong decision-making. However, in a low-group-orientation culture, such as Australia, people are encouraged to be self-sufficient and think for themselves. Leaders should be alert and aware of cultures that expect and require more collaboration.

BEST PRACTICE FOR MANAGERS IN LOW-GROUP-ORIENTATION CULTURES

Individualism is paramount in countries with low group orientation. Negative feedback may instigate negative feelings of self-esteem among individuals from such cultures. Any performance appraisal of such individuals requires the inclusion of objective measurements with specific examples, delivered in a structured way. This reduces the likelihood of poor self-esteem resulting from the dialogue, as the measurement metrics relate to specific performance rather than directly to character.

The overall success of the enterprise is understood to be important in such cultures, but it is secondary to the individual's contribution to achieving the organization's goals. Those who identify with individualism are motivated by a variable system of rewards based on personal levels of attainment. They value efficient decision-making over long meetings with much discussion. In this culture, people are encouraged to be independent and think for themselves, so feedback should reward this behavior.

- Feedback should be prepared in advance.

- Positive feedback for taking the initiative and being innovative will be appreciated.

- Positive feedback can be given face to face or in written form; individual groups value praise for their achievements, and this should be included in how employees are coached.

- Developmental feedback should include time for open-ended questions that prompt the person to develop ways to improve.

- Prepare feedback and steps for improvement but be open to cocreating solutions. Giving specific and rigid steps to progress may be taken negatively.

- It is appropriate to be concise when giving feedback, and overcommunication should be avoided. The manager should get to the point, discuss steps, and establish the required follow-up. Metrics and facts should support what is being said rather than feelings or personal traits.

BEST PRACTICE FOR MANAGERS IN HIGH-GROUP-ORIENTATION CULTURES

In cultures in which business success is primarily about a collective group effort—rather than individual attainment—any negative feedback may bring about feelings of guilt and shame.

Individuals may feel that they are "letting the team down" in efforts to meet goals.

Feedback strongly emphasizes the group's well-being rather than individual strengths and weaknesses. Those who identify with this collectivism are motivated by an equality-based system when it comes to rewards for the enterprise's success.

- Give positive feedback to the group for a job well done rather than individual recognition privately.

- Collective success for the team should be publicly emphasized.

- Action steps and areas of individual improvement should be the focus in conjunction with an acknowledgment of the person's value to the team. Use positive phrasing and give direction for progress softly and conversationally.

- Regular conversations or one-on-one meetings should be used to coach the person to success. Allow time to explore ideas and consider how the person works.

- Developmental steps and milestones should be documented. Group priorities may interfere with personal tasks and goals.

KNOWING YOURSELF—GROUP ORIENTATION

The three scenarios below relate to the cultural dimension of group orientation. The most natural response to each indicates where one may fall on the group-orientation-dimension scale.

Scenario 1

You work for a software company. One day you get a really good idea for a new product.

Response A: You decide to run solo on the start-up idea you have.

Response B: You share your idea with others you respect within the company. Your goal is to put together a group of people with complementary skill sets and then launch your idea together.

Low-group-dependent cultures encourage individuals to be self-sufficient and think for themselves (Response A).

High-group-orientation cultures believe that every person in the group must be comfortable for that team to be successful. Everyone must be heard, and this will prolong decision-making (Response B).

Scenario 2

It is close to the year's end, and your global team needs to finalize nine prominent, cross-functional user stories. You are asked to facilitate a meeting.

Response A: You schedule a one-hour meeting and send out an agenda with the open items asking people to arrive prepared.

Response B: You schedule a workshop for a full day with lunch. Because the stories touch people from several departments, everybody must have a chance to voice their perspectives. You expect to finalize the stories by the end of the week.

In low-group-orientation cultures, meetings are primarily devoted to the exchange of information and the collaboration of ideas. Decisions are expected, and people will only speak up if they have something to say. Response A would, therefore, usually be appropriate in such locations.

In high-group-orientation cultures, Response B would usually work better. A more inclusive—and therefore slower—approach will be a better method in such locations.

Scenario 3

> You have been asked by your manager to create a new business process for the sales and marketing teams.

> **Response A:** You decide that you have enough information to accomplish this on your own and will review it with the stakeholders once you've completed the business process improvement.

> **Response B:** You quickly pull a group of stakeholders together to get their input and feedback before beginning the project.

In low-group-orientation cultures, business meetings will typically be scheduled when it is time for a decision to be made (Response A).

In high-group-orientation cultures, the goal of the meeting is typically to create a forum where everyone can voice their opinion (Response B).

KNOWING TEAM COLLEAGUES

It is understanding the differences between low and high group orientation in global team situations.

Team Members

Adria (High-Group-Orientation Malaysian National)

Adria manages a call center in Kuala Lumpur (KL) for a large global company. She has several supervisors in her organization and several hundred call agents serving the Asia-Pacific region 24/7. One of the key customers in Australia recently canceled its contract, citing customer service issues, which has caused a reaction from the head office. Adria is looking for ways to improve metrics and has met with her team to generate ideas for improvement. It may take some time to solve the problem.

Oliver (Low-Group-Orientation Australian National)

Oliver is a regional manager with an international call center company based in London. He is responsible for several of their call centers in Asia, which are an essential source of revenue for the organization. The Malaysian call center has customer service issues and has recently lost a significant account. To address this issue with the Malaysian team, Oliver needs to resolve the problem before customers cancel their contracts with World Co. Oliver has just arrived in KL. He recently worked a three-month stint out of the office in India, so he feels qualified to give feedback to the KL team and to, generally, give them a "pep talk" to get performance back on track.

GROUP ORIENTATION

LOW --- / -- / - / + / ++ / +++ HIGH

Oliver   Adira

Scenario

What could Oliver do to be successful in this new role?

1. Review his cultural profile for a group orientation.

   Having completed a personal cultural profile over a year ago and spent time in India, Oliver was disappointed that his first meeting in KL flopped so badly. Citing jet lag, he went back early to his hotel. Oliver could tell he was doing something wrong in the eyes of the Malaysians, so he reran his cultural profile. He now ranked close to the middle of the "group orientation" spectrum, whereas he had been at the low end of it the last time.

2. Consider the cultural dimensions of the team, determining high and low tendencies.

   The group orientation spectrum is in play in this scenario and impacts Oliver's effectiveness. Oliver asks the managers in the call center to take the cultural assessment to understand their approach. He reviews the team profile and sets a meeting to go over the results. He will discuss the dimensions and share his story in the session, letting the team know his preferences and expectations.

3. Be prepared to flex the style.

   Oliver sees that Malaysia is at the high end of the "group orientation" spectrum and, thus, very different from him. He realizes that in his haste to address the Malaysian team, he overlooked that the firing of a colleague and the negative feedback he had given the team brought shame to the collective group. The hurried nature of the meeting did not help.

   Giving feedback in a high-group-orientation culture requires thought and planning. Address feedback to the group first, celebrate group success, recognize the team rather than the individual, and solicit ideas for improvement when performance does not meet expectations. Individual feedback should focus on how the employee contributes, or does not, to overall team performance.

4. Get outside help or coaching when needed.

   Oliver talks with a peer and asks for feedback on the situation. He learns that offering individual bonuses is not ideal in a high-group-orientation culture. Giving a reward to the team for collective positive results would have been a better idea.

5. Confront reality and move on.

   Everyone makes mistakes. Oliver realizes that the Malaysian call center manager has now lost face because of his actions. He schedules individual conversations with the Malaysia supervisors and team members to address this and asks for ideas to improve team performance.

Oliver will be honest in acknowledging that things didn't go as planned, and he will work with them to be more effective in the future. He hopes that this will "undo" the wrong first impression he has made. Oliver also plans to announce a "team building" social event outside the whole group's office. He knows he needs to flex his style by seeing the team outside the office to build trust personally.

Understanding cultural preferences will help team members understand why Oliver acts the way he does and help them see where their preferences differ. Conversely, Oliver needs to understand the team's culture to be more effective.

KNOWING WHERE

The dimension of group orientation around the world:

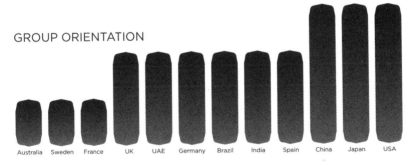

GROUP ORIENTATION

Australia Sweden France UK UAE Germany Brazil India Spain China Japan USA

LOW   HIGH

Low-Group-Orientation Culture

A country with one of the lowest group-orientation cultures in the world is Israel.

Some Cultural Etiquette Observations for Israeli Business Settings

A handshake is considered the standard greeting in business settings. However, those on more familiar terms may also place a friendly hand on the shoulder of their visiting counterpart(s). Titles and last names should be used until the Israeli takes the lead in using first names.

Israel's business environment shares many similarities with the United States and other Western nations. At the same time, Israeli businesspeople like to take time to get to know their foreign counterparts and will often socialize with them outside of office hours. During the meeting itself, Israelis tend to speak directly and will expect an agenda that outlines the purpose of the discussion. English is widely spoken in the Israeli business community, although the use of a few Hebrew words is always appreciated.

Israel's business etiquette requires foreign visitors to arrive punctually even though the meeting may start ten to fifteen minutes later than planned. Foreign visitors should offer their business card at the start of a session, and one may be requested from the Israeli counterpart in return (as it may not be offered immediately).

High-Group-Orientation Culture

A country with one of the highest group-orientation cultures in the world is Taiwan.

Some Cultural Etiquette Observations for Taiwanese Business Settings

Taiwanese culture values family, hard work, punctuality, tradition, and respect for authority and elders in society. As in the People's Republic of China—which in Taiwan should be referred to as "mainland China"—the sense of "saving face" is important, so a sense of harmony should be strived for in business settings. In meetings, punctuality is expected. Guests should wait to be introduced and then should greet the most senior person first. Handshakes are customary, and it is appropriate to give a slight bow at the same time as a show of respect (although this will not be expected of foreign visitors).

Successful business is about personal relationships, the development of which can take many years. Overseas business people should demonstrate that they expect to be involved in Taiwan for the long term—this is not, for them, a short business trip. Business visits need to be made often in order to show long-term commitment. It is necessary to keep in touch regularly from one contractual arrangement to another, rather than just reconnecting when a contract is about to expire.

Chapter 12

THE CULTURAL DIMENSION OF CHANGE TOLERANCE

KNOWING OTHERS

Cultures with high change tolerance will view change as creating opportunity and generally as a positive. Conversely, a culture with low change tolerance may believe that change might even worsen a situation that others believe could be improved by changing an existing process. They will say why fix it if it isn't broken, or we've always done it this way, so why change it now.

Societies that are high in change tolerance anticipate change happening organically. They see change as a harbinger of creativity and innovation. The level of change tolerance goes a long way toward defining how a given society views risk. Most high-change-tolerant cultures are identified by a love for innovation and for leadership spread among many individuals. Societal changes are more frequent, and creativity and experimentation are highly valued. As one would assume, the US is very high on the change-tolerant scale. However, it might surprise you to know that Germany is at the opposite end of the scale. Certainly not because they aren't innovative, but it's because they insist on doing a lot of risk analysis before making a change.

When I work with Global 2000 leaders (especially those in the US), they often complain about how implementing new business processes or restructuring a company in other countries are their biggest challenges. It's because they don't understand that every culture has a different relationship with change. The more change intolerant a culture is, the more context, rationale, and risk analysis you have to show people for them to get on board with the change. Otherwise, it won't happen, and it certainly won't happen at the speed you want it to. I work with a Fortune 50 client based in the US, and I have just completed a series of workshops designed to help their leaders in low-change-tolerant cultures get on board with the changes they are making to their new client implementation processes. The US leaders were expecting that the leaders in Germany, the UK, and India would embrace the new process and even appreciate the change. After months of them stalling the process and things not moving, it became obvious that something in their approach was broken. All it took was a series of workshops that helped both sides understand that change tolerance is very different from country to country. We created team profiles for each leader, so they could actually see where the disconnects were happening. We then showed them how and where to flex for maximum performance. They could have saved so much time and money had they done this from the beginning. Again, it's because leaders have no idea how much of an impact culture has on every single part of the business.

Societies that are high in change tolerance tend to experience higher worker turnover in businesses and organizations and accept different ways of living more readily. Societies that are low in change tolerance typically experience more company loyalty and view change as a threat to traditional ways.

Change tolerance is personal and deeply rooted in the culture of a business and society. A person with a low tolerance for change will typically work hard to document risk and is often seen as a very valuable employee. This individual may, however, be seen as an impediment to moving the business forward in a culture that sees change as a positive for growth.

In high-change-tolerant cultures, change is always associated with positive movement. In contrast, low-change-tolerant cultures may see differences as overall risky and untried.

BEST PRACTICE FOR MANAGERS IN LOW-CHANGE-TOLERANT CULTURES

Feedback should be straightforward to avoid ambiguities that the recipient could wrongly interpret.

- Positive feedback should be given either via email or in person. Recognition programs should be used, if available. These are typically more highly valued in low-change-tolerant or traditional cultures.

- It is necessary to understand that the recipient may be nervous or upset about developmental feedback, particularly when asked to change their work style. Provide reasons for the requested change and highlight benefits. Ensure that they understand the value.

- Feedback should be prepared in advance.

- Outcomes should be agreed upon, with follow-up in writing.

- Regular meetings should be set up to coach the person to reach the desired performance level.

- Positive feedback should be provided when changes are accepted, and rewards should be given for small steps.

BEST PRACTICE FOR MANAGERS IN HIGH-CHANGE-TOLERANT CULTURES

Cultures with a high-change-tolerance index are more comfortable with risk and uncertainty than those that avoid such circumstances. Organizations in highly change-tolerant locations have relatively few internal rules and regulations.

Giving feedback in such cultures requires flexibility in discussion. Allow the recipients a measure of freedom to express themselves. Innovation is welcome in such a culture, so the feedback recipients should be allowed to suggest any ideas they may have—regarding the operational or company goals—as part of the discussion.

- Positive feedback for innovation and creativity should be given, as this is highly valued.

- When giving developmental feedback, time should be allocated in order to brainstorm ideas for improvement.

- Listen with empathy and look for ways to create mutual success; a rigid approach will not be well received.

- Trust and improved communication can be built by allowing time for questions and suggestions. People with high change tolerance look for new ways of doing and improving.

- Out-of-the-box thinking and creative solutions to problems should be rewarded with positive feedback and recognition.

KNOWING YOURSELF—CHANGE TOLERANCE

The two scenarios below relate to the cultural dimension of change tolerance. The most natural response to each indicates where one may fall on the change-tolerance scale.

Scenario 1

You are working on a large project. The project is almost ready to launch when your manager decides to shift direction and includes several large changes in the project.

Response A: You feel that this is a risk to the project, the timeline, and the company's success. While you respect your manager, you make a point to prepare a detailed report that highlights the risks to the project's success.

Response B: You find this change exciting and challenging. You update the road map for your project to include the new features and tout the benefits of this change.

Low-change-tolerant cultures typically see change as risky, untried, and negative. Therefore, Response A would be well regarded in such locations.

However, in high-change-tolerance locations, such actions may be seen as slowing down the growth of the business. Change is usually seen very positively, so Response B would be appropriate in such locations.

Scenario 2

The company you work for was acquired by a large corporation.

Response A: You are worried. The leaders do not have a firm strategy or clear vision of what this acquisition means to people like you. Will you become invisible? Will you keep your job?

Response B: You are thrilled. Not only is the new owner a very successful company, but you see this as a great opportunity to move up in the ranks. You make sure to introduce yourself to your new coworkers and trust that the leaders will determine the strategy.

Organizations in low-change-tolerance cultures are more likely to favor the "wait and see what happens" approach. Response A is applicable here.

Organizations in high-change-tolerance cultures view change as a means of self-improvement, both for the business and the individual. Response B is, therefore, more appropriate here.

KNOWING TEAM COLLEAGUES

Understanding low and high orientation of change-tolerance differences in global team situations.

Team Members

Doug (High-Change-Tolerance-Orientation American National)

Doug is an American manager working for Green Chemicals and works at the global headquarters in Houston, Texas. He is known for his straight-forward communication style and his ability to get things done. Due to the retirement of his long-serving predecessor, Doug has just been promoted and given responsibility for the Northeast Asia region. He has not worked directly with this region before. To meet his goals, he will need to manage the acquisition and get the new office in Japan on board.

Shuzo (Low-Change-Tolerance-Orientation Japanese National)

Shuzo is a senior manager based in Tokyo. He has worked for a global company for many years; Green Chemicals is now acquiring his company. He is from Japan, having studied and spent his entire career there. He is very proud of his high tenure with the company and is loyal to the firm. Shuzo manages a large team and has very high trust in them. His team is nervous about the acquisition, job security, and working methods.

CHANGE TOLERANCE

Scenario

Shuzo has learned that his new manager, Doug, will be coming to Tokyo to meet with him. The purpose of the trip is for Doug to introduce himself and outline the impact of the acquisition on the company's operations in Asia. Shuzo is feeling slightly apprehensive about all the changes. With Doug's pending visit, he is concerned about how to present himself and let Doug know he is trustworthy and experienced.

How can Shuzo prepare for the meetings with Doug?

1. Review his personal cultural profile.

Shuzo completes his personal cultural profile, which aligns with Japanese cultural preferences. He learns that Japan and the United States are on nearly opposite ends of the change-tolerance spectrum. Knowing this enables him to reflect on his approach and prepare for this first meeting.

Shuzo understands that while Doug may feel at ease, he himself is uncomfortable with change. He decides that he will need to have an honest conversation and get as many details as possible on the acquisition. His team has many questions, and he wants to answer them after this meeting.

An American like Doug will likely have different cultural preferences than a Japanese manager working in his native country. Reviewing personal dimensions allows you to prepare for conversations and flex your style to be more successful when meeting with people from other cultures.

2. Consider the change-tolerance dimension.

    By understanding this dimension, Shuzo can prepare for the meeting and understand that what seems meaningful to him may seem quite ordinary to Doug. Shuzo determines what steps he needs to achieve his goals for the meeting.

    People in low-change-tolerance cultures may feel nervous about meeting new and different goals. They may be less likely to ask clarifying questions and feel offended or embarrassed if called out individually for perceived failures or not meeting goals. It is good practice to step outside your comfort zone and flex your style to make sure you have a two-way conversation.

3. Take the culture into account.

    Shuzo receives an email from Doug that expresses the company's appreciation for the years of service he has dedicated so far. The email comments on the value that Shuzo brings to the team and lets him know that the meeting is taking place to explain the forthcoming changes. Doug confirms the time and date of the meeting in Tokyo and lets Shuzo know that there will be ongoing video meetings after Doug returns to the United States. He also advises that he will be making a second trip to Tokyo.

Shuzo responds to the email to confirm goals and details. He plans to prepare in advance by creating a list of questions for Doug, and he will expect clear goals and expectations for performance to be an outcome of the meeting. Shuzo should let Doug know his preferred way of working during the meeting. If Doug does not document meeting points, Shuzo should do so.

Setting clear expectations before the meeting helps reduce ambiguity. Shuzo needs to prepare in advance because he knows that Doug will have a different approach to the significant changes and may have yet to consider many of the items that the Japanese managers will want to know.

4. Flex the style.

Staying quiet and respectful with his new boss will not help Shuzo build the trust needed to give and receive feedback effectively. He needs to flex his style, ask more questions to be more comfortable with the changes, and establish rapport and trust with Doug. He will need to provide feedback to Doug in the future. For Shuzo, this may be a very different way of working and will require extra effort to flex his style.

One of the most significant errors global managers make is to treat all discussions the same way. Adapting the method of communication, such as setting an initial face-to-face meeting to get the relationship off to a good start, allows a leader to build trust and set clear expectations.

Low-change-tolerance cultures will be less inclined to ask questions and challenge the changes; therefore, they should flex by preparing questions in advance and finding ways to build a relationship. They should step out of their comfort zone, ask for more clarification, and provide feedback on ideas and plans.

KNOWING WHERE

The dimension of change tolerance around the world:

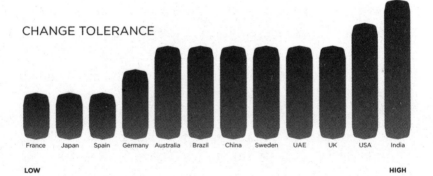

CHANGE TOLERANCE

France   Japan   Spain   Germany   Australia   Brazil   China   Sweden   UAE   UK   USA   India

LOW   HIGH

Low-Change-Tolerance Culture

A country with one of the lowest change-tolerance cultures is Italy.

Some Cultural Etiquette Observations for Italian Business Settings

In Italy, greeting one another with a firm handshake is the norm. It is necessary to shake hands individually with everyone in the group, upon both arrival and departure. In business gatherings, one should use titles when addressing others unless invited to use first names. Therefore, it is appropriate to use *Signor(e)* (Mr.) or *Signora* (Mrs.), plus the surname, when one is introduced to Italian executives. Business visitors are usually introduced first to the most-senior participants and women. The younger generation of Italians is less formal and uses titles less frequently.

Punctuality is less important in Italy than in some other countries. While it is necessary for the foreign visitor to arrive on time for an appointment, it may be a while before the meeting starts. Business cards should be translated into Italian on one side. Eye contact should be maintained in meetings. Italian counterparts may place themselves more closely to their overseas visitors than is the norm in some other countries. Business negotiations may well take place over lunch, usually longer than the foreign visitor is used to. Refusing an invitation to a business lunch or dinner is considered disrespectful. Business gifts should only be given to an Italian counterpart once the overseas visitor has received one first.

High-Change-Tolerance Culture

A country with a relatively high tolerance for change is the Philippines.

Some Cultural Etiquette Observations for Filipino Business Settings

In the Philippines, a greeting can take on different forms. Foreign businessmen will offer a firm handshake at each introduction and meeting with other men. Foreign businesswomen may initiate a handshake with both men and women. This is allowed since business is the focus. Otherwise, men and women do not normally touch or exhibit physical contact. When addressing others, one should use titles and last names unless invited to do otherwise. When exchanging business cards, the visitor should offer their card first. The gesture may not be reciprocated unless the visitor is of an equal or higher rank to the card recipient. In meetings, punctuality is appreciated in the Philippines; however, being fifteen minutes late for business lunches and dinners is not an issue.

In business negotiations, foreign visitors should be prepared to move at a slower pace than what may be the norm in their home country. This is because the Philippines is also at the high end of the relationship-dimension scale. Therefore, the building of personal relationships is critical to business success in that country. Time should always be given for social dialogue before and after the actual business discussion in the Philippines.

VIGNETTE: LIFE AND CAREER OFTEN COME
TOGETHER: A STORY OF FRANCE AND QATAR
By Guillermo Gonzalez-Prieto,
Global Leader in International Talent and
Mobility in the Argo Industry, Spain

Returning from the summer holidays to my Madrid office, I was informed that the company wanted to separate from me after several years of working with it (in IT and HR functions). This termination opened up the opportunity to relocate to the company's Paris HQ, but only with a guarantee of a three-month employment contract. Relocating to Paris with a wife and two young sons without knowing if that international experience would conclude or continue was a risk. Choosing to be brave and take the chance played out in my favor, and I ended up with a local French contract.

The higher salary was, of course, empowering—but even more so was the encouragement and support of the management and my colleagues. This inspired confidence in myself that had been hidden for many years. So, during my time in Paris, I came to discover the pleasure of managing projects remotely and nurturing an international network.

For this reason, setting up a new global mobility program for the forthcoming merger of two large telecom companies (one based in France and one in the US) proved to be an extremely joyful challenge. The trio assigned the task of designing the new program consisted of two heads of global mobility—a senior French leader who was relatively new to global mobility and a younger US American from New Jersey with a great deal of experience and ambition—and me. We were given a period of seven months to achieve this. All the work was done by conference call, as Microsoft Teams was still science fiction at that time!

My experience living in California as a teenager and my then-developed depth of knowledge of French culture caused me to assume the role of "referee" in arbitrating, negotiating, and managing the conflicts of this project. This successful project implementation gave me the opportunity to continue working in France in a larger role. I gained regional experience in assuming the management of a large team of mobility managers and specialists, who were primarily based in Egypt, France, Germany, and the UK. Managing the remote squad proved to be the easy part, whereas managing the day-to-day activities of the French team (who were based at the exact same location as I was) turned out to be quite challenging. The team was in a difficult psychological state due to prior experiences with harmful management styles, ones that involved a clashing of backgrounds and mindsets. Thus, most of my time was dedicated to managing conflict and emotional reactions every time I gave out rewards and recognition. This was taking place even as I searched for my own leadership style.

I finally realized that I didn't have to follow one particular style but instead could follow my instincts and personality. In time, the establishment of a service center in Romania—and the subsequent transfer of activities there—put cross-cultural differences at the center of the table. Traditionally and historically, the French company had never had a fair opinion on and recognition of diversity. This opinion worsened even more when the use of "diversity" implied the acceptance of the very opposite views and values of Eastern Europe (notably Bulgaria and Romania). At the same time, communication was stiff on the one hand and confusing on the other. One team would manage cases on an ad hoc basis whereas the other team focused entirely on the rigorous application of standard company processes. The need to make the process fit in every single case—an impossible task in this particular area of HR activity—made the French teams particularly angry and frustrated.

Some years later, I moved from a chronic sector in crisis (telecom) to the wealthier world of oil and gas services, from a low-discipline but a cost-controlled environment to one highly standardized but with extremely generous budgets. Life was suddenly all about speed and micromanagement. I saw ambitious and aggressive teams being encouraged to compete with one another. My need to decompress after office hours told me things were going too far.

Changing again to work for a national oil company in Qatar seemed like a big cultural jump, but it was relatively easy after the variety of situations I had experienced by then. I soon found the primary HR agenda to be the "quaternization" of management positions and development of local Qatari talent. Indeed, HR was instead referred to as "human capital." This term describes precisely how all the experienced expats hired there tended to feel. We knew that we wouldn't have career opportunities—as these were all reserved for the Qataris—but, on the other hand, we could benefit from a very diverse environment, full autonomy, and trust in our own capacity.

In such an environment, life becomes easy—and your recognition outstanding—when you deliver on expectations and follow the innumerable list of codes, policies, and procedures. Being with an enterprise that builds a new company culture, set of values, and leadership profiles, that looks to the future and opens up to international expansion—but at the same time always pursues a "national preference"—is easy to interiorize and accept until you separate from that environment. At that point comes the realization that you have been accepting national discrimination and putting this at the center of HR priorities. Looking at the future with optimism—but simultaneously with fear—defined the environment. While most companies—and their employees—around the world were leaning toward more flexible post-pandemic business practices, the local culture of the Qatari company was unable to overcome the suspicion that employees can only perform well when under strict control. This control defined working in Qatar and was also present in many areas of one's personal life. When faced with the dilemma of choosing between flexible working arrangements, hybrid models, and full office presence, the company indulged its conservatism and fear. In doing so, it requested that all employees be back in the office every day of the week, allowing for no flexibility whatsoever.

This was what drove me to return to Spain after fifteen years away. So now, when I am asked, "What is your home country?" I can respond with much wisdom but never a clear answer!

Chapter 13

TURNING THE UNDERSTANDING OF CULTURAL DIMENSIONS INTO TEAM EFFECTIVENESS

UNDERSTANDING THE DIMENSIONS OF CULTURE—AND their variations—in societies forms a large part of the ESG equation. Maximizing one's own CQ—or cultural intelligence—level is a vital ingredient in achieving this. CQ indicates a level of personal awareness that transcends unconscious bias and even the dimensions themselves.

Many assume that contact with those from different cultures will increase CQ automatically. We have seen in previous chapters, however, that CQ can be affected by the implicit beliefs that individuals hold about a foreign culture and that it requires an awareness of self and a willingness to fully "sit in someone else's shoes."

At the far end of the scale are those who believe that cultural characteristics are unchangeable and are thus likely to develop what academics call the "intercultural rejection sensitivity" syndrome. Researchers of this condition suggest that such a pessimistic attitude undermines the ability of individuals to adjust to cultures other than their own, as it can reinforce biases and, therefore, block any CQ development. While such individuals are unlikely to be active in high-visibility roles in an agile international enterprise, business leaders should know that such a phenomenon exists.

ENHANCING CQ AT THE PERSONAL AND TEAM LEVEL

We have seen in previous chapters that cultural inclusion journeys are as diverse as global culture itself. Each one is a unique reflection of the individual's personal background and life experiences, as well as the multiple and varied locations that may be involved. Above all, a "trifecta" of attitudes needs to be maintained.

1) Remain aware of the importance of cultural intelligence.
2) Remain conscious of one's own unconscious biases.
3) Remain curious about other cultures, both from the get-go and when new cultures may be added to a complex team structure.

There are some general guidelines that can turn these attitudes into successful team cohesion.

Clarity and Simplicity of Language

One example of a powerful communication norm is to use clear and simple language, avoiding slang, sports talk and other non-inclusive analogies, and colloquialisms. An HR leader learned firsthand the importance of preventing sports analogies in global-team communication while meeting with a senior leader from Germany who was reviewing a presentation. One of the slides in the deck was titled "On Deck." Confused, the German leader asked, "What does 'on deck' mean?" A team member explained the baseball analogy and then changed the slide title to "What's Coming Up Next."

Such interactions are virtually inevitable; however, a heightened awareness can eliminate confusion by using culturally shared terms rather than make one party feel uncomfortable when a lack of context renders a term confusing.

Sensitivity to Time Zones

Global leaders should consider the impact of working across different time zones. In the spirit of creating a culture of inclusiveness, leaders could establish norms that encourage teams to share the "time zone burden." Setting up conference calls with participants who work in the US, Europe, Asia, and Australia can be particularly challenging. In many organizations, conference call scheduling tends to favor US-based employees. For example, India-based employees may need to be available for conference calls from six o'clock in the evening to two o'clock in the morning in order to collaborate with their US-based colleagues. This work schedule does little for team cohesion and engagement.

Flexibility in Working Hours

Leaders and employees in global roles may have learned the "follow the sun model," meaning that they work with Asia at night when the sun rises in the east, with Europe in the morning, and with Latin America and the United States in the afternoon. This work pace is often not sustainable over time. Therefore, it is necessary to provide some flexibility for team members so that they are not working around the clock.

A C-level executive with over thirty years of international business experience shared, "It is important to be aware that simply being on a multi-time-zone call is not a guarantee of an ability to contribute, especially if one is expected to participate very late at night or extremely early in the morning. In my situation, sometimes a very late-night call is immediately followed by a very early morning call the next day. When scheduling, it is important to consider the ability of participants to be mentally alert and fully participating, not just physically present."

Meeting Norms

Teams need to set meeting norms that are clear and well-understood by everyone. For example, one approach asks that each person take ownership of creating the agenda, facilitating meetings, and taking notes. This method fosters accountability and engagement for each team member. After meetings, the person who facilitates the meeting sends a summary of the key points and actions discussed to everyone on the team to check for understanding and ensure accountability.

A global leader shared these tips for implementing meeting norms. "I recommend that everyone use active listening concepts in meetings. After a meeting, they should ask for feedback to confirm if everything is understood...Be aware of appropriate conversational pacing, tone of voice, use of interruptions, and lengths of pauses because they vary by culture, and be adaptable to the differences." Additionally, people in certain cultures may feel awkward providing feedback. Therefore, it is helpful to ask open-ended questions, such as: "Yoshi, how would this work in Japan?" This approach opens the door for dialogue in such a way that the person providing feedback does not feel as though he is being rude.

Many global leaders encourage their teams to use virtual tools during meetings. This approach can enhance collaboration and the quality of interactions by offering a multisensory experience and creating stronger relationships. When people see each other, even when using virtual technology, the quality of interaction can be enhanced, humanizing the experience.

Communication Methods and Frequency

People in some cultures prefer dialogue (in person or on the telephone); others prefer email communication, which gives them time to digest the words and reflect on a carefully worded response. For example, people in a French workplace often prefer discussion and debate, while a Dutch workplace approach is often seen as more to the point. Of course, these are broad generalizations, and the experience can vary greatly. Therefore, it is essential to observe and avoid stereotyping. For example, after the merger of the French and Dutch national airlines, Air France executives were surprised by the frank observations made in public by their counterparts from KLM Royal Dutch Airlines.

Additionally, maintaining a high frequency of communication and "touch points" often becomes significant. A global leader shared, "I have weekly touch points with direct reports on my team and also monthly one-on-one calls with employees deeper in the organization. Sometimes it's important to 'over-communicate' to reinforce a feeling of belonging to an organization." Clearly, there is not just one method or style that this multifaceted leader employs. He explained his reasoning, saying, "These communications become the baseline for developing a clear understanding of the team's objectives."

Building Capacity for Cross-Cultural Competence

Organizations need a road map, or strategy, to build capacity for cross-cultural competence within their leadership-development curriculum and talent-management initiatives. To build capacity, effective organizations need to establish the right mindset, skill set, and tool set. The goal is to move people along on the continuum from "knowing" to "doing" to "being." A recommended approach is to consider the following three stages of development.

Stage 1: Create a foundational level of cultural awareness by providing a common, consistent, and shared language (such as cultural dimensions) around understanding cross-cultural differences. This goal could be achieved using knowledge-based virtual sessions that scale across the organization to build individual effectiveness. The target groups would likely be first-time global leaders, employees, and HR business partners (HRBPs).

Stage 2: Provide an in-depth understanding of cross-cultural differences by building individual self-awareness. This transitional stage allows global leaders and team members to further develop their skills through assessments, individual development planning, and new leader and new team assimilations, as outlined below. The target groups would likely be experienced leaders with global responsibilities, global teams, and high potential who are likely to take on global roles.

Stage 3: Develop a more in-depth use of models, tools, and frameworks embedded in talent-management initiatives designed to build cross-cultural competence through leadership coaching. Participants are expected to "pay it forward" by supporting colleagues new to the cross-cultural experience through mentoring, networking, coaching, role-play, and business case studies, as illustrated below. This step has the added benefit of driving scale and consistency across the organizational approach. The target groups would likely be senior global leaders, including expatriates, with extensive global responsibilities, for example, general managers' responsibilities in multiple countries.

Activities	Definition
Cultural Assessments	Tools used to heighten awareness in areas critical to interaction and working effectively with people from different cultures
Individual Development Planning	The process of identifying goals, outcomes, and action plans in the context of developing cross-cultural competence

New Leader Assimilation	Facilitated meetings between a new leader and his or her team to accelerate organizational learning for the new leader in a cross-cultural context
New Team Assimilation	Facilitated meetings intended to build capacity for growth and change within global teams by focusing on the ability to recognize behaviors that impact team dynamics and effectiveness

THE CULTURAL-AWARENESS TO-DO LIST

- Learn more about your own specific cultural profile. Professional profiling tools are key to achieving this.

- Invite your team members to share their own cultural profiles, measured by the same professional profiling tool as yours.

- Build mutual awareness of the communication styles of your team members. Finding common ground in this area is a great tactic for creating a mutual bond and helps to develop trust and respect. It assists significantly by eliminating barriers in communication.

- Be aware that the more multicultural a team may be, the higher the need for explicit communication.

- Ask appreciative inquiry-type questions about the target culture (for example, "What is important when establishing credibility with customers here?"). In other words, it is imperative to be curious!

- Be explicit about your own style (for instance, say, "I'm typically direct/indirect") and use the neutral vocabulary of the profile to describe cultural differences.

- Build in time to connect informally, such as setting up a coffee break (live or virtual) with a team member (or members) in the target country (or countries), so as to learn more about their preferences and norms.

- Ask for feedback on what you are doing well and how you can improve at regular intervals from your team members in the target country.

- Build solid local relationships in a culturally appropriate way.

- Be frequent in communications in order to stay visible virtually.

- Be prepared for meetings and for participating with the group.

- Discuss what "on time" means for meetings and deliver on time or communicate early about delays.

- It can be useful for a leader to create a bio sheet (indicating the years of experience with the company and industry and what the leader brings to the project and/or team), to be used either formally or informally.

- Create ground rules and team norms in meetings that balance participation and comfort levels with silence.

- Build in time to give feedback on what is working and what can be improved in your team communication, either one-on-one, via surveys, or in team meetings, on a regular basis.

- When in doubt, ask for feedback, summarize, and recap.

IN SUMMARY

Today's global work environment is the new normal. It is virtually impossible to work in a modern organization without experiencing some degree of impact from varying parts of the world. Ignoring the effect of multiple time zones and cross-cultural communication challenges is no longer an option. To be effective in this increasingly global context, we need to rethink our view on leadership based on building effective future global leaders. Global leaders need to become advocates of reframing the leadership perspective on cross-cultural competence.

Leadership-development curricula and talent-management initiatives need to address the challenges of working cross-culturally. To make lasting changes, development and training programs must include cross-cultural competence as a requirement for anyone assigned to global work teams. These programs should offer diverse methodologies and tools that can reach more people by building social and structural bridges. By creating forums for meaningful dialogue on cross-cultural differences, organizations can change from within as they grow to be more globally effective.

By encouraging cultural diversity and creating a "space" to enhance cross-cultural skills, we will attract a more diverse and inclusive workforce that is equipped to handle new challenges on the horizon. In doing so, we will embrace the best that diversity offers, learning from one another and growing our organizations to be truly global in an increasingly global workplace.

Leaders of global teams may want to explore scalable and sustainable digital solutions such as https://www.worldtraderesource.com/products-services/goworldwise that will serve the needs of the entire organization, minimizing costs in time and money and maximizing the learning potential.[12]

Chapter 14

ANOTHER STORY: SOMEONE WITH PARENTS FROM TWO VERY DIFFERENT CULTURES

By Sabrina Gill Kent, Executive Vice President at the National LGBT Chamber of Commerce of the United States

"AND FOR THE FRIEND?" IT was the first time that I could remember realizing I was different. It was the first time I was an "other." The server, I don't believe, meant any harm. We were sitting in a dimly lit booth at Stonewood Grill, and my childhood best friend came to dinner with my dad and me.

I'm half Punjabi and the only daughter of my mother, a first-generation immigrant. My dad—fair, blond-haired, and blue-eyed—scarcely resembled the dark skin, brown hair, and brown eyes displayed on my mom's side of the family. So, at the restaurant, the server believed that Kathleen, with her light skin, had to have been my father's daughter. The impact didn't strike me then; it was only as I grew older that I recognized that this was a core memory. As a kid, I was offended and territorial—"That's *my* dad!"—and, as an adult, I realize that it subconsciously clicked then that I wasn't white, something I hadn't really known. It's these seemingly little moments that have such an impact—while they may not define our lives, they inextricably shape them.

I grew up in an upper-middle-class neighborhood in Florida. While Florida is a melting pot of different ethnicities, the Orlando suburb we lived in was predominantly white, and the magnet schools I went to—bookending four years in a mostly white private school—were the clearest examples of the multiculturalism that existed outside of the confines of the bubble I was brought up in.

I grew up in Lake Mary, so attending Seminole literally required crossing the railroad tracks into Sanford, where there were few gated communities, lower socioeconomic status, a perception of higher crime, and a more diverse population.

Before attending Seminole High, I went to Lake Mary Preparatory School, and it was there that I remember wishing with my entire body and soul that I had been born white. At LMP, I was one of several brown students in a class of about sixty. Our self-esteem as preteens and teenagers is so deeply affected by the kids around us, and my experience was no different.

I was about twelve when it clicked for me that white was the equivalent of beautiful (societally speaking, of course). I was exotic, and, to this day, people who don't know any better love to label me as "ethnically ambiguous."

Growing up, I felt undesirable. I thought I would never be the girl who others had a crush on. It may seem trivial to some, but, to a young girl, what her peers think of her is close to everything, and society teaches girls that beauty is the highest indicator of worth. For me, the repercussions of those ideals have manifested in several harmful ways—abusive relationships, disordered eating, and nicotine addiction, among others.

I'm eternally thankful for voices like my mom's, who constantly reminded me that I was not just beautiful but also intelligent and self-sufficient, that my worth was not tied to how other people viewed my looks.

My mom knew firsthand what it was like to be "other," and she had to make space to define her own worth in a society that wouldn't do it for her. At the age of eleven, my mom left India for Canada, a place she had never visited, where she would have to learn a language that she did not yet know. My mom and her siblings would be the few brown kids at school and in their neighborhood. Little girls would tug on my mom's long braided pigtails and make fun of the food she ate.

Within a year of moving to Ottawa, my mom would learn English and excel in school, particularly in science and mathematics. She'd skip a grade, graduate early, and head off to university. She would meet her future husband, controversially marry a non-Indian by twenty-three, have my brother, and work to put her then-spouse through graduate school. In the early eighties, her spouse had a string of unfaithful encounters that would lead to divorce.

My brother would then be raised by my mom, who did so without financial support from my brother's paternal parents or from my mom's own parents. She put herself through a master's program, so poor that she would choose to pay for diapers rather than buy food for herself. In 1991, my mom hired my dad for a project she was leading. After several months, they started dating and got engaged. This would be the second non-Indian my mom would marry. At this point, I think her parents were just relieved that she was marrying at all—and they loved my father and his family.

I was born in Ottawa in 1993. By the late nineties and early 2000s, my mom was a senior project manager in the IT field, at the height of her career, excelling as a top earner and performer in a male-dominated field. If there is any question as to where my ambition comes from, one can look no further than my mom to find the answer.

As a result of her work, my mom traveled a lot. Shortly after we moved to the US from Canada, she maintained a contract working for Ontario's Ministry of Transportation and would be gone for two weeks at a time. Other than extended visits from my *nani* (maternal grandmother), exposure to the Punjabi side of my family was scarce. Most of them lived in California and Canada, so visits happened infrequently.

Sitting around the dinner table with either side of my family, though, made one thing ultimately clear—I was too white to be brown and too brown to be white. Through no fault of my family, this distinction felt so plainly evident to me. While I wasn't raised speaking Punjabi, the influence of my mother's culture in my upbringing provided a stark contrast to that of my father's side of the family.

On my mother's side, my cousins were immersed in Punjabi culture throughout their entire lives. One of my older cousins affectionately referred to me as her "little half baby." When meeting Indian people in the world, there is a clear sense of relation— and a clear understanding that we live two very different experiences of our culture. I feel like somewhat of an imposter.

When meeting non-Indian people, particularly white people, I also know I don't fit in. Our ideas of family and culture are incredibly different. I am a chameleon who simultaneously belongs nowhere and everywhere, and that can be a strength.

At sixteen, things started to come into perspective. I spent a significant amount of time working to convince myself that I wasn't gay because being gay wasn't an option. I'd stay up at night with the weight of coming to terms with my identity sinking into my chest. It's important to note that stigma alone is what caused me to battle with my LGBTQ+ identity. I was not raised in a family that taught me being gay was wrong. My dad was agnostic, having been raised as a Christian in the United Church of Canada, and my mom was raised Sikh but identifies as spiritual. At a young age, I felt alienated from many of my peers who were actively involved in their church communities, so I begged my parents to let me join my friend's youth group after they let me go once.

My parents told me that when I was old enough to make an informed decision, I could choose what I believed in. They said that as long as I was a child living in their home, I would not be joining the youth group, but they were happy to let me go that one time. To this day, I feel that this is one of the greatest gifts I received as a multicultural child.

Being free from the confines of religion allowed me to pursue my own moral and ethical code, informed by many different faiths and systems of belief, and, as an LGBTQ+ adult, I do not carry the weight of religious trauma for loving whom I love or identifying as I do. Thank you, Mom and Dad.

As a freshman, I went into my first year at Rollins College thinking that I could be straight. I was so very wrong. It took me all of four days to come out to Breanna. We met on day one of freshman orientation, and everyone said, "You won't stay friends with the people you meet now." Joke's on them because we are best friends to this day and live twenty minutes from one another in Colorado. I confessed to Breanna that I'd just broken up with my girlfriend—who, for days prior, I'd been referring to as my "best friend"—and I was heartbroken. Breanna had been telling me a lot about her "best friend" from home too. It would be a few weeks before she confessed that her "best friend" was also her ex-girlfriend. Being heartbroken over the breakup with my girlfriend confirmed what I did not want to be true—I was gay, and no amount of pretending to have crushes on boys in my dorm was going to change that.

By Thanksgiving, I'd come out on campus, was on the board of the Rollins LGBTQ+ student group and wasn't hiding my lesbian identity from anyone—but my family.

I was starting to feel secure in who I was, so the time had come. Mom invited me to brunch, and I thought I'd take this opportunity to tell her who I really was. She beat me to the punch. As she glanced up and over her menu, Mom made eye contact with me, which she only does when she's trying to pull the truth out of me. "So, you're a lesbian?" I replied with the single most awkward yep of my life.

While my mom is by no means the model of a traditional Punjabi wife or mother, she, like so many of us—and sometimes unknowingly—carries the weight of her cultural upbringing into every facet of her life. This is what it means to be the child of immigrant parents, and I wouldn't change it for anything.

This influence has helped me deeply understand the value of time, people, family, and connection in ways I likely would not have otherwise understood them; this is part of what makes me the chameleon I am. But when I was coming out, the weight of my mom's culture was a heavy burden to bear—for both of us.

At that brunch, my mom reminded me that I'd been a girly girl my whole life, that I had long hair, and that I was still hyper-feminine—there was no way I could be a lesbian. I imagine my mom's idea of a lesbian at that time was a leather-jacket-toting woman with a buzz cut and Harley. All these things, including questions about whether I could have kids one day or maintain a decent job, I could handle; it was the next thing she said that cut sincerely.

"As long as your *nani* is alive, you can never get married."

It struck me then that my mom, though unready to accept me as a lesbian (and I can't blame her—coming out is a process for parents too), was mostly unprepared for what her family would say. She would be a failure in their eyes, and so, over the course of the next year, little moments would arise in which it was clear she was discouraging me from being who I am.

When I told my mother that I was on the board of our LGBTQ+ student association, she became concerned I'd never get a job with that on my resume. A few months later, I started dating Grace. She was less than thrilled and constantly reminded me that my guy friend Joel with his kind heart and mild manners was such an excellent fit for me. Throughout all this, coming out to my dad was a stark contrast. I never did come out to him, actually. My mom told him, and when she did, he laughed and asked, "What did you expect, sweetie?" He had known all along and had made sure I knew that he was okay with it too.

Over time, things have changed. As I said, it's a process for parents, and my mom has always prioritized my happiness. She supported me when I received a scholarship to go to DC the summer before my senior year to intern at the LGBTQ+ association I've now worked at for nearly nine years. She is the first to defend our community and by all means is the Pride-flag-waving parent who openly supports me and my partners. She has mourned losses for our community and grieved when LGBTQ+ people lost their lives at Pulse and Club Q. She has voted to protect us, and she has become an incredible ally.

While I never did come out to my *nani* while she was alive, nothing about my queer identity is a secret on my mom's side of the family, and I recognize that my coming-out experience has been so much better for me than it is for so many others.

As a gender studies minor, I read Uma Narayan's *Dislocating Cultures: Identities, Traditions, and Third World Feminism* and gained deeper insight into national values. Narayan is also Indian and a person of multicultural experience.

The United States' national values are independence, freedom, and liberty. The national values in a place like India are family and community, so it's no wonder that my mother was concerned about what her family thought of her parenting and hoped that my being queer was just a phase.

Time, in America, is currency. Time is money, after all.

In the US, you arrive in this life one day, and once you've lived this life, it is over; this is why we say, "Time is the only thing you can't get back," and why the most disrespectful thing someone can do is waste your time. This is why, in business, we work to accomplish as much as possible in the shortest amount of time. "That meeting could've been an email," right?

My dad was raised a military brat. If he wasn't five minutes early, he was late. In her personal life, not her business life, my mom is perpetually running ten to fifteen minutes behind her stated departure time. In her mind, there is no need to have anxiety about something as minute as time. Growing up, my mom always ensured that we'd sit down and eat dinner as a family. We would take our time. When guests came over, dinner may have been served at seven or seven thirty in the evening, but there was no rush.

At my grandma Sandra's house, things were different. Everything happened on time and according to plan. Being on time constituted a sense of pride—and anything short of being on time was a sign of disrespect.

In Indian culture, which Hinduism in prominent part influences, time is cyclical. It has no beginning and no end, so when I went to India for the first time on a business trip in 2017, I was prepared for cultural differences.

In India, it became clear to my American colleagues that meetings would last about twice as long as they do Stateside. Before diving into business, our Indian counterparts wanted to know about us as people. The saying that "people do business with people they like" carries significant weight in India. It's about trust.

And success is a large part of Indian values. In a caste system, social hierarchy is of the utmost importance. Maintaining a good job as proportional to one's caste is also significant.

When visiting the Indian headquarters of a US-based multinational company, we sat down with the head of Diversity and Inclusion (D&I) for the company's in-country operation made up of more than two hundred thousand people. After about forty-five minutes of the conversation focused on getting to know one another, this individual shared that our work in supporting the LGBTQ+ community was dear to him. He had started at this company working in IT over ten years earlier. At that time, he was closeted and would use his personal time off to attend the company's LGBTQ+ employee resource group (ERG) events. On his day off, he was spotted by his boss in the lobby of their building. His boss saw his company Pride lanyard, commented on liking it, and asked, "What are you doing here on your day off?"

He responded that he was actually on-site to attend the ERG event, and his boss asked why he would take time off to do such a thing. He replied that he didn't think he would be accepted— it was then that his life changed. His boss told him that it was unacceptable that he felt as though he was working in a space that wouldn't accept him, and even more so that he was using his personal time to participate in the company's ERG.

Fast-forwarding, this individual became the head of D&I at this company, and his acceptance at work entirely changed his view of himself. He was able to come out to his family and be accepted with open arms because his family knew he wouldn't lose his job or livelihood; he wasn't forced into an arranged marriage with a woman he would never truly love; he was able to bring his best self to work; and he is now working to make this company an even more inclusive space than it was when he found it.

Discrimination at work is a retention issue; it encourages turnover by diminishing productivity and job satisfaction, and it also has long-term consequences on the mental and physical health of employees. We are talking about covering in many respects for fear of retribution, whether actual or perceived. A Human Rights Campaign study called "The Cost of the Closet and the Rewards of Inclusion" found that 35 percent of LGBT employees feel compelled to lie about their personal lives at work.

The case for inclusion is simple—inclusion affects the bottom line. In addition to recruitment and retention, inclusive workplaces with high-performing employees result in better financial outcomes and stock performance.

It's this kind of workplace acceptance that contextualizes my own experience. When I jumped into my career, I learned quickly that as a young woman professional, I was often the only woman in the room—or the only brown woman in the room. This developed into a kind of imposter syndrome. Am I really qualified to be here? Should I share the idea that's on my mind? If I present an alternative solution, am I being too forthright? Am I always the progressive voice in the discussion?

Too white to be brown, too brown to be white, too straight-presenting to be queer, too queer-presenting to be straight. Being a chameleon can be a privilege and an asset; this allows me to enter different places and spaces under the radar to affect some sort of change along the way. But this is something that is learned, not innately known.

Chapter 15

A GLOBAL INCLUSION JOURNEY

THROUGHOUT THIS BOOK, WE HAVE demonstrated how enhanced cultural and social awareness benefits businesses and organizations. This has been seen to apply equally to the enterprise as a whole and to the individuals within it. Cultural and social inclusion has a direct impact on the success of leadership teams, employees, and suppliers, and this, in turn, is reflected in the bottom line. We live in an era of irreversible globalization. As such, national governments also realize that promoting cultural awareness and inclusion can enhance the productivity of an entire country. Productivity can be defined as the measuring of the efficiency of production of goods or services. Therefore, increased productivity can raise the living standards of an entire nation.

In this chapter, we will first look at ten nations that support cultural awareness with active policy-making. All enjoy high levels of productivity in global terms. We will reflect on cultural and social awareness and inclusion initiatives at the national level and how they have been instrumental in achieving increased productivity.

MAPPING THE INCLUSION JOURNEY FROM THE INDIVIDUAL TO THE NATIONAL LEVEL

It is no accident that several countries we will highlight are in the European Union. Over many years, the EU has adopted measures to protect disadvantaged members of society, both in and outside the workplace. An example is the Strategy for the Rights of Persons with Disabilities 2021–2030. These measures empower persons with disabilities to participate fully in society and the economy throughout the member states.

The objective of the strategy "is to ensure that persons with disabilities in Europe, regardless of their sex, racial or ethnic origin, religion or belief, age or sexual orientation," will:

- "enjoy their human rights";

- "have equal opportunities" and "equal access to participate in society and economy";

- "are able to decide where, how and with whom they live";

- "can move freely in the EU regardless of their support needs";

- and "no longer experience discrimination."

The countries highlighted below pursue active inclusion policies at the government level (although, in the case of the United States, the private sector tends to take the lead). They all simultaneously report some of the world's highest levels of productivity.

1) *United States*

The Migrant Integration Policy Index ranks the United States first out of thirty-one assessed countries in terms of antidiscrimination laws and protection. The United States also ranks high on the access-to-citizenship scale, and legal immigrants enjoy suitable employment and educational opportunities. However, many of the nation's inclusion initiatives have been pioneered by the private sector and, therefore, vary company by company. The United States regularly ranks in the top six globally in terms of productivity.

Example of legislative measures in the United States

In 2004, Massachusetts became the first US state and sixth, world jurisdiction to legalize same-sex marriage. Following this, opponents of same-sex marriage began tightening marriage restrictions throughout the country, with several states approving state constitutional amendments explicitly defining marriage as the union of one man and one woman.

In 2008, California and Connecticut both legalized same-sex marriage, followed soon by Iowa, Vermont, and New Hampshire. Up until 2012, legalization was enacted through state courts and legislation, or as the result of the decisions of federal courts. In 2012, Maine, Maryland, and Washington became the first states to legalize same-sex marriage through popular vote.

On June 26, 2015, in the landmark civil rights case *Obergefell v. Hodges*, the Supreme Court ruled that the fundamental right to marry is guaranteed to same-sex couples by both the due process clause and the equal protection clause of the Fourteenth Amendment to the United States Constitution.

In December 2022, the United States Congress passed legislation to enshrine same-sex marriage rights into law and grant gay unions federal protection. The result is that while same-sex marriage ceremonies may not be legal in every state, those who were married in a state that *does* recognize same-sex marriage have the same rights no matter where in the United States they ultimately reside.

Example of corporate measures in the United States

Citigroup is an American multinational investment bank and financial services corporation. The enterprise has programs designed to foster career opportunities for everyone, cultural diversity in the workplace, and inclusion. Diverse perspectives are being sought at all levels of the company in order to improve performance and boost employee engagement. Citigroup's enterprise-wide approach to setting inclusion goals encompasses all employees, including specific recognition of military veterans and those with disabilities.

Novartis is a major American Swiss pharmaceuticals enterprise. The company strives to pursue a diverse hiring policy. Novartis maintains a constant focus on pay equity, disabilities, inclusive leadership, and unconscious bias.

Salesforce is an American software company. The enterprise's inclusion initiatives are based on four pillars: people, philanthropy, policy, and purchasing. Salesforce maintains several key performance indicators related to the pillars. These include the goal of doubling the US representation of black employees in senior leadership roles by the end of 2023. Salesforce is committed to a 25 percent year-over-year growth in spending on minority-owned businesses.

A direct correlation exists between a feeling of inclusion at the individual level and the national performance of certain countries. Such success starts at the corporate level via specific initiatives that may or may not be supported by governmental measures. This is concurrent with the large-scale remodeling of team structures within international businesses, an approach that has been the primary legacy of the COVID-19 pandemic. This has heightened the urgency and need for leaders to fully understand themselves and those with whom they work.

2) Belgium

Belgian workers benefit from a degree of automatic wage indexation higher than that of most other advanced industrialized nations. The nation also offers access to unemployment benefits more generous than that of many similar countries. These policies exist to strive toward a society where no one is "left behind." This causes Belgium to score better than some other EU countries in terms of inequality. These measures were implemented to enhance social inclusion at the national level. As a result, Belgium regularly ranks as one of the world's ten most productive countries.

Example of legislative measures in Belgium

In 1996, Wallonia (the French-speaking administrative region of the country) became the first to issue a decree setting integration priorities for thirteen years (followed by a second decree). Both were designed and implemented by the regional Centers for Integration and through local initiatives carried out by public services or nongovernmental organizations. The top three priority areas were and remain:

- social cohesion within an intercultural society;
- equal access to services;
- and social and economic participation.

A third decree in 2014 introduced an integration program (*parcours d'intégration*) with over one hundred hours of French language training, along with twenty hours of citizenship training and professional orientation. The program became mandatory for newcomers in 2016.

In 2004, the interior ministry of Flanders (the Flemish-speaking administrative region of the country) was the second to design an integration strategy. The five-year document was implemented by local reception offices and organized Belgium's first compulsory integration program with four priorities:

- social orientation, including values and norms;
- active citizenship, including rights and duties;
- Flemish as a second language;
- and employment.

Other plans followed and were implemented at different levels of government: a regional agency for civic integration, local language-learning organizations, and reception offices. The top three priority areas were and are:

- to fight against ethnic divide and the weak educational attainment of developing nation nationals;
- to improve equal access to services;

- and to increase the knowledge of Flemish as a second language.

The capital region of Brussels has had a migrant integration strategy since 2017. It implements a compulsory integration program with the following top three priorities:

- citizenship training;

- Flemish or French as a second language;

- and social and economic participation.

However, given that Brussels hosts both the Flemish- and French-speaking communities, the legislation not only of Brussels but also of the Flemish- and French-speaking administrative regions coexist there.

Example of corporate measures in Belgium

Solvay is a Belgian chemical and plastic manufacturer and is one of the nation's largest employers. The CEO leads a company-wide forum to support inclusion. Solvay has a permanent task force dedicated to this, led by a head of Inclusion. The task force develops and articulates Solvay's overall strategy and influences change throughout the organization. Executive sponsors and ambassadors support and work within employee resource groups (ERGs) and Inclusion catalysts to help advance program initiatives. Individuals throughout help shape, embed, and uphold inclusion across the group on a constant basis.

3) Denmark

Denmark generally experiences low levels of unemployment. Those who are out of work are usually entitled to some form of social support from the government. Significant numbers of people from within the European Union migrate to Denmark for work purposes. Some 10 percent of the Danish national population hails from outside the country (two-thirds of whom are from non-Western countries). The combination of a strong economy and active integration policies is resulting in fewer cases of discrimination in the workplace. More immigrants speak Danish than ever before, with 50 percent of male refugees entering the workplace within three years of arrival. While maintaining a generous welfare system, Denmark is one of the seven most productive countries in the world.[13]

Example of legislative measures in Denmark

Denmark is known for its comprehensive legislation that supports inclusion within society. In 1989, Denmark was the first country in the world to grant legal recognition to same-sex unions in the form of registered partnerships. The first Danish minister for gender equality was appointed in 1999. As a result, a cornerstone policy was the Gender Equality Act of 2000. It provided for the promotion of gender equality, including equal integration, equal influence, and equality in all functions in society on the basis of women's and men's equal status. It counteracts direct and indirect discrimination on the grounds of gender and prevents sexual harassment. Denmark's first female prime minister took office in 2011. Denmark legalized same-sex marriage in 2012, and same-sex partners are treated by law in the same way as opposite-sex partners.

Example of corporate measures in Denmark

Maersk is Denmark's largest employer and is one of the world's major shipping companies. Respect for diversity—no discrimination against any employee—is a core value at Maersk. The company recognizes that facilitating a culture where everyone feels comfortable, respected, and fairly treated provides access to a larger, more diverse talent pool. According to their website, Maersk's official diversity target is to have—throughout the enterprise—at least 40 percent of management positions held by women and at least 30 percent owned by those from an ethnically or socially diverse background by 2025.[14]

4) France

Policies and programs supporting social inclusion are advanced in France compared to those of many countries. The government strives to balance national competitiveness with relatively high social contributions made by both individuals and employers. France routinely ranks within the top eight global economies in terms of productivity. The national productivity rate is some 25 percent higher than the EU average.

Example of legislative measures in France

Being a secular republic, France rejects any official categorizations of ethnic, linguistic, national, or religious minorities. This concept is based on the idea that the government should interact with every individual in order to give equal treatment to everyone.

Simultaneously, however, the French Labor Code states that it is forbidden to punish or dismiss employees; to exclude potential employees from the recruitment process (both external and internal); or to cause employees to endure direct or indirect discriminatory measures within a private or public enterprise on the basis of their age, ethnic or racial origin, gender, marital status, medical condition and/or disability, name, nationality, physical appearance, political opinions, religious beliefs, or trade union activity.

Moral and sexual harassment is prohibited by law in France and perpetrators are subject to fines and/or imprisonment.

Private companies and public bodies with more than twenty employees must have workers with disabilities account for 6 percent of their total workforce. Employers are provided with three options to meet this target: hiring disabled workers as employees; subcontracting workers from the sheltered sector; and paying a contribution fee to an organization dedicated to furthering professional inclusion of the disabled in the private sector.

Example of corporate measures in France

Sodexo is a large French company in the field of food services and facilities management. Sodexo is at the forefront in France of companies with an inclusive hiring strategy. According to their website in late 2022, 55 percent of all Sodexo staff members are women, and 58 percent of the members on the board of directors are female. The company maintains gender-balance networks throughout its global operations. As a result of these and other measures, Sodexo has seen its worldwide employee engagement increase by 4 percent, its brand image strengthen by 5 percent, and its gross profit increase by 23 percent in recent years.[15]

5) *Germany*

Germany experienced unprecedented levels of immigration during the second decade of the 21st century. This was in large part due to the movement to the country of many thousands of individuals fleeing war in Syria and the surrounding nations. Assisted by specific programs and government-funded financial aid—as well as Germany's dual vocational-training opportunities—integration into the German labor market has been a noticeable success. Most refugee arrivals are by now in regular employment. Germany's previous most significant wave of inbound migration was from Turkey, when the economy rapidly expanded after the Second World War. Today, some 25 percent of the German population has a migrant background, 1.5 million of whom are of Turkish heritage. Successive German governments have prioritized dialogue with the Muslim community (which includes Turks). Germany often ranks as the fifth most productive country in the world.[16]

Example of legislative measures in Germany

In Germany, support and guidance for people with disabilities are ensured by a legal framework, subject to the Basic Law (*Grundgesetz*) and the Social Code (*Sozialgesetzbuch*). Furthermore, the United Nations Convention on the Rights of Persons with Disabilities entered into force in Germany in March 2009. The national government and the sixteen federal states have taken measures to guarantee the human rights of persons with disabilities; to prevent discrimination against persons with disabilities; and take appropriate legislative, administrative, and other steps to achieve the objectives of the convention. In education, school legislation was amended to allow for the inclusion and support of students with disabilities into the mainstream education system.

Example of corporate measures in Germany

Infineon Technologies is a semiconductor manufacturer and a large German employer. Infineon corporate policy is to create a working environment free of prejudice in order to foster a corporate culture in which the benefits offered by diversity are consciously utilized and everyone can freely develop their potential in the best interest of the company. The company has adopted diversity requirements for the composition of its management board in addition to inclusion initiatives all around the world. This includes encouraging young employees to spend time in overseas divisions of the company so as to increase the overall cultural awareness of the enterprise.

6) Ireland

Ireland's productivity rate is regularly ranked as one of the highest in the world. This is driven in large part by the high number of multinationals—relative to the size of the national population—located within the country. The high rate of immigration to Ireland in the 2000s has caused it to become far more diverse. Some 12 percent of Ireland's population is composed of foreign nationals, nearly half of whom are Polish and UK citizens. The Irish government has implemented specific programs that promote the integration of migrants and encourage social inclusion. The strategy aims to promote and protect the diversity, equality, and participation of migrants in the economic, social, political, and cultural life of the nation. As a result, labor productivity in Ireland has grown at an annual average of 4.5 percent in recent years.[17]

Example of legislative measures in Ireland

The Assisted Decision-Making (Capacity) Act was signed into law by the president of Ireland in 2015. The act reformed previous legislation—which had been in place since the 19th century—in which individuals with impaired decision-making skills were universally classified as insane. The act established a modern statutory framework to support decision-making by adults who have difficulty doing so without help. The act created three types of decision-making support options (assisted decision-making, co-decision-making, and decision-making representative) to respond to the range of support needs that people may have in relation to decision-making capacity. With each of the three decision-making support options, decisions can be made on matters of personal welfare and finance/property (or a combination of both).

Example of corporate measures in Ireland

Allied Irish Banks is one of Ireland's largest employers and has a prominent role in the country's financial services sector. Since 2017, senior leadership programs have ensured diversity and inclusion education for all staff, including new hires. Ongoing outreach programs among employees include "Transitioning in the Workplace" initiatives and generally promote the high visibility of diversity and inclusion throughout the company.

STEPHAN M. BRANCH, MBA, CEO

VIGNETTE: CULTURAL DIMENSIONS AND
THEIR INTERSECTION WITH BELONGING AND
INCLUSION IN 21ST CENTURY IRELAND

*By Jim Frawley, Principal and Founder,
Bellwether Executive Development*

When speaking of Ireland, the intersection of belonging and inclusion cannot be discussed in cultural terms without addressing the past. In addition, Irish cultural norms aren't limited to the island, as the Irish diaspora consists of seventy million people of Irish heritage located all around the world. Given that the population of the actual island (between both the Republic of Ireland and Northern Ireland, which is part of the United Kingdom) is only seven million, the diaspora has an outsized influence both on the world and on the island.

Ireland has a unique history, primarily due to its location. Constant invasion from around the world has created a tribal culture, one primarily Gaelic with influences from the Spanish, the Middle East, the Vikings, and others. While these influences certainly have made their stamp on Irish identity, more recently (as in the last three hundred years), the primary drivers of Irish identity have been the conflicts with the British and poverty. These two drivers—philosophical and physical—continue to steer various aspects of Irish life, from politics to sports to the arts.

Hundreds of years of sectarian violence, as brutal as most other places in the world (including the most bombed hotel in Europe), has led to an ongoing battle cry that has seen the external diaspora become quite involved in internal politics. While we can often attribute exclusion to physical attributes, the difference between the Republic of Ireland and Northern Ireland was primarily philosophical and religious, whereby Catholics were not allowed to own property or work. This was paired with the physical challenge of famine and disease, which saw the Irish population drop by 25 percent due to death and emigration. The Irish built up a global diaspora, which fled an island of violence and starvation. But while the Irish diaspora may have traveled a considerable distance, it always simultaneously remained close to home.

Today, Ireland continues to reinvent itself by both desire and necessity. Brexit has left Northern Ireland behind, pushing the island closer to reunification. It has also thrust the Republic of Ireland into a unique position of power in Europe as the primary trade location between Europe and Britain. While the island is still two separate countries, the violence has slowed, thanks to the work of initiatives like Project Children and the resulting Good Friday Agreement, which led to a cease-fire between the Irish Republican Army and the United Kingdom. Foreign investment and growth in technology-related industries have created a new economy. An increasing flow of migrants from Africa, the Middle East, and Eastern Europe are building a true melting pot in places such as Belfast, Dublin, and Galway, reshaping what it means to be Irish.

Membership in the European Union led to the movement of people to the island of Ireland—on both sides of the border—from other member states, predominantly from the countries of Eastern Europe. This in itself changed the composition of Irish society. In the case of Northern Ireland, the presence of tens of thousands of—for instance—Polish nationals in Belfast can be seen as a "lotion" to soothe the persistently sectarian nature of the city's human makeup.

Meanwhile, the 2022 census in Northern Ireland revealed that, for the first time in history, those identifying as Catholic are in the majority. Traditionally, this part of the population has favored leaving the United Kingdom to unify with the Republic of Ireland. The Good Friday Agreement stipulates that a referendum on unification must happen if the majority of the population of Northern Ireland wants that choice (in other words, a referendum about a referendum). While the result of either referendum is not a given, the exit of the United Kingdom from the European Union has thrown the dice in the air in a manner that would not have otherwise happened.

These are not small changes, and with change comes significant challenges. What was once primarily a disparity in philosophical identity is now also becoming a physical difference, presenting new challenges to inclusion, equity, and access, from housing to employment. The Irish have a reputation for resiliency and being welcoming. The island is considered by many to be ripe for a successful reunification that will merge with a broader global influence as the culture evolves.

Three questions remain:

- What will it mean to be Irish in the 21st century?
- Can Ireland unify peacefully, and do the two regions want to? Or do they want to remain two separate countries?
- Will the diaspora keep up with the new Irish identity, and what does inclusion mean beyond the Irish border?

Due to demographic, economic, and political influences, national cultures inevitably evolve with time. The cultural identity of Ireland is evolving more uniquely than most, as the cultural norms traditionally applied to the island have become more fluid. At the same time, Belfast remains a place with a "peace wall," which closes every night and separates the Protestant and Catholic communities. More is to be seen on the future of Ireland. At the moment, it is a prospect that is as fascinating as it is unknown. What *is* known is that the rise in international permanent residents of the island of Ireland—and the Irish diaspora around the world—will constitute a unique aspect of the inclusion and equity component of the new Irish culture of the 21st century.

HISTORICAL EXAMPLES OF DIVERSITY IN THE IRISH HIGH OFFICE

For a large part of the 20th century, the Republic of Ireland derived much of its cultural norms from the Catholic Church, as the church historically served—over previous centuries—as the primary source of the nation's "non-British" identity. As a result, the country was known more for its traditional values than as a global "trendsetter" in embracing diversity. However, in the last years of the 20th century and the early part of this century, Ireland provided the world with some high-profile examples of how cultures and nations evolve.

In 1990, Mary Robinson became the first female president of the Republic of Ireland (or *Uachtarán na hÉireann*). Then, in 1997, Mary McAleese succeeded her and remained in office until 2011. For the first time, women were representing the Republic of Ireland as its head of state on the world stage. Furthermore, in 2017, Leo Varadkar became the country's prime minister (or *Taoiseach*). This was significant in that he is half-Indian and openly gay; therefore, his appointment was seen worldwide as further testimony to the advancement of diversity in Ireland. Varadkar became prime minister once more in December 2022. He will serve in the role until the next general election in Ireland, which is currently scheduled for March 2025.

UPPING THE GAME IN TODAY'S BUSINESS WORLD

The quest by business leaders to obtain organizational efficiency—as well as economies of scale—has led to the involvement of an exponentially more-significant number of diverse global locations in the final composition of corporate teams. Managers who had never before had to think about things beyond their national environment suddenly find themselves coping with the direct responsibility of team members in other countries—and even different continents.

This has inevitably put individuals to the test, whether based in a home location considered to be a "global" city—such as London or New York—or somewhere that experiences far less routine exposure to the outside world, an example of which would be the headquarters of a multinational company located in rural Germany or the US Midwest. Wherever the person is sitting, the challenges of running a global team remain the same. The ability of the manager to cope with these challenges will, of course, depend on the location involved. This is the "obvious" part of the scenario. The far more imperceptible aspect of the equation is the fact that the ability of the manager to "flex into" their new responsibilities depends equally on their own life story. In today's remote world, this is the case no matter if managers have had any personal international experience themselves.

Senior leaders of international organizations must recognize this if their new team structures are to thrive in the long term. John A. Powell, director of the Othering & Belonging Institute at the University of California at Berkeley, observes, "International managers may not all play the trumpet or violin, but they now need to help people to be able to play together successfully."

An international team can be defined as "a group of people who work interdependently with a shared purpose across space, time, and organization boundaries using technology." Virtual teams may be composed of members from vastly different cultures, working in geographically diverse—and possibly distant—locations worldwide. This creates hazards and obstacles in communication processes that can cause personal conflicts and threaten the level of trust between members or the remote manager. Language barriers can also influence team communication on many levels, even beyond the basic comprehension of the group's chosen language of communication. At the emotional level, language barriers can intensify a feeling of frustration and/or isolation among some team members. However, if it is handled correctly, these elements of diversity can cause teams to be more curious and open and, thus, more innovative.

Primary elements of cultural diversity around the world have been highlighted earlier in this book. The business leader working with colleagues from disparate cultures needs to flex his or her approach. As we have seen in earlier chapters, when dealing with—for instance—team members from collectivist cultures, it can be valuable to stress their significance to the success of the team effort. Concurrently, team members from more individualistic cultures need to be specifically given acknowledgment for their actions. Even such a simple flex as that can make all the difference.

As well, the cultural intelligence of the leader has significant implications for team members. The technical environment and nature of work in virtual teams are uniquely challenging. Studies have shown that the best candidate for a global virtual team member may be a person who can combine collectivism with a high tolerance for change. Team members from more direct communication or low-context cultures may be better prepared to collaborate in a virtual environment. Such individuals can often feel inherently more satisfied—and, therefore, more efficient—than their peers from more high-context cultures.

Cultural competency creates great opportunities for managers and employees to improve their performance ultimately enabling team members to better reach their global potential. Successful global virtual collaboration is becoming increasingly crucial as employers compete for virtual team workers. Although such are the changes in the post-pandemic workplace, companies must look at themselves more profoundly than they had previously, focusing on their practices and policies regarding language and intercultural training. Post-pandemic success requires deep corporate self-understanding.

Businesses are in the process of redefining their ongoing business practices worldwide. This is the case whether the headquarters of an international company is in the Bavarian countryside or the middle of Manhattan. Given the permanent nature of the post-pandemic business world, the time has come for organizations to now look at how to bring durability and stability into—and, therefore, add strength to—the equation.

Companies are now opening up their cultural and social landscape, promoting awareness at the C-suite level and among employees at all levels. The key to achieving enduring success is the implementation of organizational policies and processes that maintain awareness moving forward. The whole perception of—and attitude toward—corporate inclusion is finally being accepted as a critical element of business survival. It is generally accepted in the business world that diverse companies not focused on diversity and inclusion do not perform as well as those that are. Active diverse companies often hire the best talent and boast more engaged employees with a sincere "sense of belonging" to the enterprise. As we have observed, this is also being understood—and acted upon—by more national governments.

The large numbers of remote workers that we now see in wildly diverse locations around the globe give business leaders a responsibility to implement diversity and inclusion into their company culture wherever possible. After that, it is essential to continuously educate and maintain core values of inclusion to ensure sustainability. As already mentioned, the global pandemic caused most businesses to consider their approach to inclusion. However, whatever the backstory, values related to diversity and inclusion will remain at the forefront of company decision-making worldwide. In an increasingly globalized business arena, effectiveness in communication and action is imperative. Companies that are not diverse underperform in every industry sector. In today's harsh global business environment, a lack of internal diversity can jeopardize the very existence of an organization.

Chapter 16

WHERE ACADEMIA MEETS CULTURE AND INCLUSION

By Helen Newman

Academic research methodologies that teach precision also have enough room for openness when it comes to DEI. Researchers are trained to review and analyze data without expectations. While one might speculate about answers to questions, the process of the scientific method exists specifically to leave space to uncover alternate theories, and sometimes, conclusions counter to the original hypothesis. From that complex lens, one used by the academic researcher, the data scientist, we look at examples of how DEI has shifted from what had previously been a more universally accepted understanding of "diversity" often meaning a visual representation flirting with the line of tokenism, to something more thoughtfully inclusive. By expanding the collective awareness for a more encompassing understanding of diversity, one that also links the well-suited pairing of equity and inclusion, we can better comprehend the importance of incorporating and championing acceptance and belonging into an environment.

Recognizing and properly identifying an organization or institution's culture versus the climate is at times overlooked. Often an assumption is made that they are one and the same when rather they influence and impact one another. An institution may take for granted that everyone operating within the shared company culture is experiencing the climate in a similar or similar enough way. While culture is wrapped around a set of shared norms, values, beliefs, attitudes, and customs, a climate is about the atmosphere itself. How the environment is felt by people within a group stemming from the culture created. Various groups and people experience the same atmosphere differently and thus the climate can impact individuals and certain groups more or less profoundly. Without having an accurate read on the climate it becomes harder for an organization to implement changes and alter the collective thinking.

When any new group enters an environment the culture of an organization needs to adapt. A good example for academia has been welcoming Gen Z (and soon to be Gen Alpha[1]) to our campuses. As we have done so, higher education as an industry had to learn how the generation defines themselves, which often materialized in more complex and complicated ways than their predecessors. Gen Z is after all the most racially and ethnically diverse[2] generation in US history. The different social identities and areas this generation expresses include but are not limited to gender, race and ethnicity, sexual orientation, social class, socioeconomic status, neurodiversity, (dis)abilities, religion and religious beliefs, and academia. The systems that support these

1   McCrindle, Mark, and Ashley Fell. "UNDERSTANDING GENERATION ALPHA." Australia: McCrindle Research Pty Ltd, 2020, https://generationalpha.com/wp-content/uploads/2020/02/Understanding-Generation-Alpha-McCrindle.pdf.

2   Mitchell, Travis. "On the Cusp of Adulthood and Facing an Uncertain Future: What We Know About Gen Z So Far." Pew Research Center's Social & Demographic Trends Project (blog), May 14, 2020, https://www.pewresearch.org/social-trends/2020/05/14/on-the-cusp-of-adulthood-and-facing-an-uncertain-future-what-we-know-about-gen-z-so-far-2/.

students must continue to evolve. In our efforts to support this evolution, academia must simultaneously progress and ask questions like, how does higher education challenge itself to become more inclusive to not only recognize these different identities, but do so deeply throughout an institution or across the industry? Further, what role and/or responsibility do universities have to buttress the growing diversification of social identities?

Consider the "duty of care responsibility" institutions of higher education have compared to that of an international corporation or NGO. While the corporation will have their global mobility teams monitoring and making adjustments and, in some cases, expanding the definition of that care for their expats on international assignments, the duty of care academia has to students also needs to further develop when educating and supporting their intellectual, social, and behavioral development. In higher education the duty of care must also incorporate some safeguards or protective measures and guidance as many of these undergraduate students are considered emerging adults and are of the traditional college age of twenty-five or under.[3]

3   National Center for Education Statistics. (2022). Characteristics of Postsecondary Students. *Condition of Education.* U.S. Department of Education, Institute of Education Sciences. Retrieved October 2, 2022, from https://nces.ed.gov/programs/coe/indicator/csb.

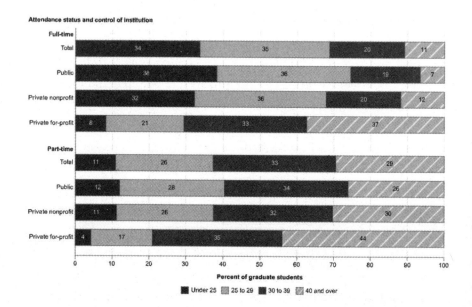

Attendance status and control of institution

	Under 25	25 to 29	30 to 39	40 and over
Full-time				
Total	34	35	20	11
Public	38	36	19	7
Private nonprofit	32	36	20	12
Private for-profit	8 / 21	33	37	
Part-time				
Total	11	26	33	29
Public	12	28	34	26
Private nonprofit	11	26	32	30
Private for-profit	4 / 17	35	44	

Percent of graduate students

■ Under 25   ▨ 25 to 29   ■ 30 to 39   ▨ 40 and over

Over two decades ago, Dr. Jeffrey Jensen Arnett, world-re-nowned researcher and Clark University psychology professor, identified a new development stage for individuals aged from eighteen to twenty-nine. This group became known as emerging adults. In the research, Arnett argued that in Western cultures, for those that allow people in their late teens to mid-to-late twenties, periods of extended independence, such individuals are still in a place of identity formation. Hence much exploration occurs across many spaces for the traditional university student. In attempting to fulfill the higher educational duty of care to the emerging adult population it becomes critical to have a deeper and more robust understanding of who these students are and how they self-identify so the levels of support can best align with their needs.

The same holds true in the workplace. Not only are corporations and organizations employing emerging adults, but some emerging adults are also even creating their own organizations, companies, and start-ups. Learning to identify the employee population beyond a database of identity markers originating from their initial hiring documents or how one appears physically in the workplace is a crucial step in expanding awareness and reframing what actually is diversity. Further, educating the community so a more extensive shared viewpoint and comprehensive understanding exist will lay the foundation for shifting the culture and climate journey ahead.

Universities and colleges have their own unique ecosystems and putting a new group such as Gen Z into the population requires new thinking and an openness to adjust as the system itself will inevitably be changed by this addition. The larger the institution, the more complex a network and interconnected the systems become from within. Without staying abreast of the institutional climate the new population experiences, how can an institution fully prop up this cohort? In looking at the ways to support Gen Z in higher education, learning who they are, how they experience the current institutional climate, and what is important to them for their own growth and development becomes essential.

Much has already been written about Gen Z and their overall generational values, behaviors, and attitudes as well as their consumer habits. These digital natives as they are known and their preferences are still regularly being researched today. According to Roberta Katz, senior research scholar at the University of Stanford's Center for Advanced Study in the Behavioral Sciences

(CASBS) and co-author of *Gen Z, Explained: The Art of Living in a Digital Age*, "A typical Gen Zer is a self-driver who deeply cares about others, strives for a diverse community, is highly collaborative and social, values flexibility, relevance, authenticity and non-hierarchical leadership," so comprehending the importance of how and what diversity means to this generation becomes a basic first step in creating a universal DEI lexicon.

In academia, we are taught the value of using a mixed-methods approach for societal and behavioral research. We learn to evaluate, assess, utilize proper tools for data collection, understand the context for what is being asked, and try to comprehend where participants are coming from prior to the start of a project. Deploying a mixed methods approach, one combining elements of both qualitative and quantitative research, often helps to uncover a complete picture of the landscape being investigated or question(s) being asked. Thus, it would make sense that higher education might look at and come to accept that there are different entry points for everyone into the DEI space. Starting with this basic acknowledgment has helped the industry propel itself forward and support our institutional communities and various populations.

Accepting the reality that different entry points exist alone is not enough to influence organizational culture, but it is a place to begin. If an organization truly wants to successfully create and foster a community that is interconnected globally, anchored in shared norms, and utilizes universal ethical principles while acknowledging a diverse set of cultural expressions, what formula or road map is there to follow? As the field continues to mature in this area, world-ranked international higher education institutions such as New York University (NYU) have found staying committedly focused on primary actions of change can aid with the ongoing transition. Working cross-sectionally throughout the organization to consistently demonstrate a commitment to **valuing people, investing in training**, and **welcoming nontraditional cultural innovation** have been the most effective tools for expanding and pushing the collective community's growth mindset.

While there is no one-size-fits-all approach to changing organizational culture and alerting the climate around DEI there are elements and actions organizations and leadership within the institutions can employ to create a deeper awareness and provide more space for mental growth. One particularly successful tactical method taken at NYU has been to create a framework, one where learning DEI across all spaces of the educational ecosystem is a shared responsibility. More recently, the push for collective responsibility has been a shift in thinking from where DEI had previously sat, often solely in institutional Human Resources departments. This is the case across the industry as more and more schools are creating formal DEI institutional senior leadership positions. Again, taking a shared organizational responsibility approach to DEI, regardless of industry, nurtures and encourages different perspectives and voices to be heard and ideally amplified. Thereby raising concerns and issues that may not have been adequately identified or addressed in the past.

Creating the shared responsibility for DEI learning is a larger macro need within the institution as a whole and must be felt and meaningfully encouraged consistently throughout. Some actionable and achievable goals for expanding an organizational culture framework may include:

1. **Identify** and obtain an accurate assessment of the current landscape (both the culture and the climate).
2. **Promote** the change desired by educating the community about where the organization is going, why, and how the former pathways were insufficient.
3. **Develop** institutional support for the culture shift across and in all layers of the organization.
4. **Build/Commit** to new structures and resources to continue the necessary ongoing promotion of DEI throughout the entity.

Identifying and understanding the current landscape will require thoughtful data collection and a self-acknowledgment that more questions than immediate answers will likely surface. Such as what are the available instruments and assessment tools the organization has access to, are new or different resources needed, and might an outside group be better suited and more objective to collect the discovery data rather than the organization or institution itself? How to meaningfully use the data? Which groups within the organization will have access to and review the data to help determine paths forward? How open or willing might participants be in sharing or reflecting on their personal experiences around DEI within the organization? How to protect what data is shared during the discovery period? What data does the organization truly need? How open is leadership to learning and uncovering information that they may or may not be ready for? What will leadership do with the data and are those intentions shared with participants at the onset? How will the organization validate the data and pinpoint the necessary organizational actions post-collection?

While answers to these questions will vary by institution and organization the more open and prepared leadership and the community are to experience the assessment and learn the outcomes the easier the initial shift or expansion should be. Ideally, the data discovery approach should take a holistic feel and be as considerate to as many primary and secondary organizational stakeholders as possible. Meaning, all levels within the organization should have an opportunity to share their perspectives so the results are layered and more encompassing of the entire environment.

Think of this step as taking an organizational diagnostic of where the landscape is for various stakeholders. By taking this diagnostic and communicating with the community about the intent before assessment deployment, the organization has a chance to frame what will be happening in the coming weeks, months, or years. Illustrating the institution's commitment to **valuing people, investing in training**, and **welcoming non-traditional cultural innovation**.

Higher education is fortunate to be in a space where data-driven decisions are part of the ethos, as are reflecting on best and next practices while focusing on learning and engaging growth mindsets. After conducting the assessment and evaluating the data learned during the discovery period, a healthy institution can begin to identify different areas of concern. Those areas then become the future organizational goals and objectives for the entire community to promote. The promotion of these goals will be better received and translated if a cross-sectional approach is applied.

Educating the community about where an organization is headed in the now and the future is a critical step to building proponents of and for the upcoming changes. Explaining the why is helping to lead those who may otherwise be dismissive of the need for the changes. Taking the opportunity to reflect on where the organization may have been in the past can also be a helpful, strategic approach to acknowledging and highlighting the contributions of the former and current guard while simultaneously building the space for inter-generational alignments. In this step, it is equally effective to be vocal about the areas that require improvement and/or in some cases, areas where obvious deficiencies exist.

Similar to NYU's approach to DEI or GIDBEA[4] (Global Inclusion, Diversity, Belonging, Equity, and Access) researchers at the NeuroLeadership Institute (NLI)[5], including CEO and co-founder Dr. David Rock, argue that with a company's deep commitment to building new organizational structures and committing the resources long term, it is possible for an organization to change their culture in nine to twelve months. NLI posits that the fastest way to change a culture is by altering our human habits. Understanding the new priorities, creating genuine habits that support the new priorities, and having systems that bolster all are the keys to success. Assisting people to support their own best habits and those for the organization can prosper by making

---

4   "Global Inclusion and Diversity." New York University, 2023, https://www.nyu.edu/life/global-inclusion-and-diversity.html.

5   "Your Brain at Work." NeuroLeadership Institute, October 18, 2020, https://neuroleadership.com/your-brain-at-work/latest-from-the-lab/?paged=2.

an effort to scale learning into compelling information and using methods like storytelling with frequent reiteration. Sharing and resharing the new priorities little by little is often more effective for memory recall. Further, helping people learn new insights with a peer or two can be a useful approach. Storytelling where data is presented to explain the "how and the why" of culture shift (new priorities) is happening can be a powerful, memorable, and non-confrontational way to receive said data.

How do other industries and spaces in society handle the shifting organizational DEI culture shift? How do they support the expansion and deepening of DEI and assist with growing the collective's understanding of the field? In the spring of 2022, the US Department of State announced that the US passport would begin allowing for the use of a third gender option or an X identi-fication,[6] thereby enlarging the former, more limited binary male or female gender selection on the official passport application form. Regardless of one's own personal opinion about the subject matter, the decision and allowance the US government made creates a more formal space for historically marginalized minority communities to receive recognition and acknowledgment.

The US is not the first country to make this change. According to the Migration Policy Institute many countries around the world, including Australia, Bangladesh, Canada, Denmark, Iceland, India, Malta, Nepal, New Zealand, and Pakistan, have allowed for a non-binary gender passport selec-

---

6   United States Department of State. "X Gender Marker Available on U.S. Passports Starting April 11." Accessed October 10, 2022. https://www.state.gov/x-gender-marker-available-on-u-s-passports-starting-april-11/.

tion.[7] Austria, Germany, and the Netherlands are also looking beyond the binary lens. The gender identity issue is but one area where an expansion of society's mind can create a more inclusive experience for others.

Michael Wiseman recently published a piece on growing and measuring inclusion in the workplace. Wiseman highlights how Gartner,[8] a multinational research and consulting company, did an extensive project surveying almost ten thousand employees worldwide. This research identified seven dimensions and practices of inclusion. The more employees regardless of their industry felt these dimensions from and at their companies the higher the inclusivity of the organization.

1. **Fair treatment**: opportunities for advancement, rewards, and recognition exist across the organization
2. **Integrating differences**: different opinions are respected
3. **Decision-making**: consideration given to ideas and suggestions from other teams
4. **Psychological safety**: acceptance of expression of true feelings at work
5. **Trust**: open and honest communication is received from the organization
6. **Belonging**: people and the institution as a whole care and value the employees
7. **Diversity**: leaders and managers are diverse as well as the institution itself

---

7   Quinan, C. L. "Rise of X: Governments Eye New Approaches for Trans and Nonbinary Travelers." migrationpolicy.org, August 15, 2022, https://www.migrationpolicy.org/article/x-marker-trans-nonbinary-travelers.

8   "Get to Know Gartner." Gartner, 2023, https://jobs.gartner.com/why-gartner/.

Ultimately, what Gartner found was that organizations that create spaces where the workforce feels the dimensions above are viewed by the employees as ones that are more inclusive. To create a greater culture of inclusivity, organizations need to have employees experience (the organization's climate) these elements regularly and see consistent reinforcement of said values (reinforcing the organization's culture). Taking a localized diagnosis of both the culture and climate is critical to the success of an institution's implementation of new policies and attitudes to expand the collective organization's thoughts around DEI.

As an institution focuses on developing deeper and creating more inclusivity in the workplace by expanding and helping individuals better understand diversity as diversity goes far beyond the visual differences, equal attention must also be paid to shifting the nomenclature and creating a shared organizational vocabulary. For example, helping the community be able to identify the difference between equality and equity. At NYU, the community is consistently reminded that equity is different from equality and is more of a process that requires taking different people's needs into consideration alongside histories of oppression and disenfranchisement. in order to distribute resources and create opportunities accordingly.

In 2016, artist Angus Maguire created the below image for the Interaction Institution for Social Change (IISC)[9] to help individuals visually comprehend the difference between equality and equity and why giving everyone the same resource, in this case

---

9   "Let's Fight the Return of the Old Normal." Interaction Institute for Social Change, March 20, 2023, https://interactioninstitute.org/.

a box to stand on, is not the same as recognizing different individuals' needs so all can have the opportunity for the experience.

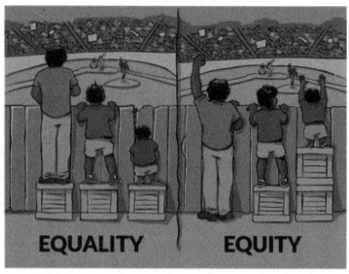

Interaction Institute for Social Change | Artist: Angus Maguire

As richer inclusion and equity efforts legitimately become more embedded in a culture, the climate by which individuals feel seen, heard, and supported can help to foster a stronger sense of belonging.

NYU is fortunate to have Dr. Lisa Coleman[10] as the head of New York University's Office of Global Inclusion (OGI). She is the inaugural Senior Vice President for Global Inclusion and Strategic Innovation for the institution. Dr. Coleman returned to NYU after helping to shape Harvard's and Tufts' DEI spaces. Her

10   "Lisa Coleman, Phd." NYU, 2023, https://www.nyu.edu/about/leadership-university-administration/office-of-the-president/global-inclusion--diversity--and-strategic-innovation/lisa-coleman.html.

voice and compelling perspective on belonging are beginning to take form throughout our global network.

Here at NYU, Dr. Coleman and the OGI office are helping the community not only better define the concept of "belonging" but also see how such can be operationalized on a global institutional level. Additionally, she is pushing us to reframe the concept of "new normal" often utilized in the immediate post-COVID pandemic period to "new different." As she argues, a "new different" is an opportunity to make transformative, sustainable, equitable changes to systems as opposed to accepting reverting or accepting the status quo.

Dr. Coleman reminds us that "belonging is an action" and when done well, belonging operates empathetically within an organization and integrates the process of learning and openness to debate. Helping to ultimately attain accelerated innovation and possibilities. The community has to be receptive and aware that conflict will happen and such presents opportunities to transform the institution's practices focusing on a more equitable, co-created, inclusive, and diverse experience. Conflict is part of a transformational process. In her own words, "belonging integrally includes contestation without expulsion or obliteration," meaning when an organization has a healthy culture of belonging, individuals and groups can have those deep discussions and disagreements, and are able to share their views without having to worry about their perspectives being dismissed, ignored, undermined, and receiving (perceived or more overtly) negative and immediate or future effects as consequences to the debate.

If organizations can learn to leverage the assets of differences (viewpoints, opinions, and experiences) as opposed to receiving those differences and the issues raised as "problems to solve or fix" they have a better chance of creating a more harmonious climate where individuals from various social identities feel welcomed to share, encouraged to suggest, and can create a culture of improvement and innovation. The use of design thinking can aid an individual's ability to be ready for differing opinions, viewpoints, and perspectives when all are brought to the table for dialogue dissection.

Stanford's Hasso Plattner Institute of Design School[11] suggests five phases of design thinking: Empathize, Define, Ideate, Prototype, and Test (*Interaction Design Foundation, CC BY-SA 3.0*). These five phases are similar to the actionable and achievable goals noted previously and applying such simultaneously can create a more holistic approach to expanding the DEI culture of an organization.

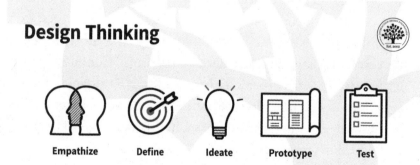

Design Thinking

Empathize   Define   Ideate   Prototype   Test

Interaction Design Foundation
interaction-design.org

---

11   The Interaction Design Foundation. "What Is Design Thinking?" Accessed January 3, 2023, https://www.interaction-design.org/literature/topics/design-thinking.

1. Empathize: Research the needs
2. Define: State needs and problems
3. Ideate: Challenge assumptions and create ideas
4. Prototype: Create solutions
5. Test: Try out solutions, repeat, and refine

The best research projects are those crafted with a mixed methods approach and acknowledge that there is always more research, questioning, and exploring to be done. As the DEI landscape continues to develop, perhaps Gen Z and the incoming Gen Alpha populations are uniquely suited to continue the expansion of collective awareness by pushing academia and the world beyond antiquated views. We here in higher education will continue to ask questions, source and validate good data for analysis, and make our recommendations in hopes that the social consciousness extends beyond itself to better and more deeply comprehend what diversity is and can mean, along with creating more inclusive spaces while providing equity for those who have been without and supporting environments of acceptance and belonging.

Chapter 17

WHERE CULTURAL COMPETENCY MEETS CORPORATE STRATEGY

THE LACK OF CULTURAL INTELLIGENCE or competency is sometimes even more pronounced in how HR will implement its strategies, business processes, and learning models to create cultures of belonging and inclusion in an effort to increase team cohesion and effectiveness. Most global HR leaders say they have learned so much through the years by making big mistakes. Many say that they made the mistake of listening to external consultants working in the inclusion space who have told them to use a *Center-first Approach* model (which focuses on middle management, or the organization's center) to create more inclusive cultures. After investing millions of dollars in consultants over years and years of providing countless workshops, seminars, and speakers that target middle management, they realize that they cannot produce any tangible and impactful results.

One chief diversity officer and talent and inclusion leader from a Fortune 50 company experienced this firsthand and said she saw no improvement after spending years and millions of dollars using this *Center-first Approach*. She noted that external consultants are often motivated by billable hours, and, obviously, there are more billable hours to be made if a company chooses this approach. After five years with no needle movement, she decided to pivot her strategy. She said she learned that the only approach that would work was a ***Top-down and Bottom-up Approach***. She said, "You must get the C-suite engaged first."

Leaders that fully understand cultural intelligence and cultural competencies know that a ***Top-down and Bottom-up Approach***, where you squeeze the middle, is what works around the world. Middle management must recognize that the senior leadership team, or C-suite, is driving the strategy. They need to understand that inclusion is an expectation of the leadership team to truly support the vision of creating a more culturally competent culture.

However, there is another equally important piece to this approach that almost every executive leader will miss entirely because they haven't learned this in graduate school, from a book, or even through experience working in a global company. They would have needed to learn specific cultural competencies to recognize this: every country has a very different relationship with hierarchy and communication. In hierarchical cultures (and this constitutes the majority of the countries on the planet), people are taught culturally, academically, and professionally to take explicit direction from their leaders. They are trained to respect titles, positions, levels, credentials, and degrees. Leaders are expected to **DIRECT**, not **FACILITATE**. Examples of hierarchical cultures include Japan, China, Latin America, Spain, France, India, and most of Asia (excluding Australasia). That said, the ***Center-first Approach*** will never work in these cultures because people need to hear from the top that diversity and inclusion are important. Remember—they expect you to **DIRECT** them.

I recently worked with a Dutch company. The Dutch are very egalitarian, as are the Swedes, Australians, and most US Americans. This Dutch company refused to understand why a **Center-first Approach** wouldn't work, as they have become more global. They wrongly assumed that the rest of the world is egalitarian as they are. And it didn't help matters that their head of diversity and inclusion was a US American (and thus also low on the hierarchy scale). Very few cultures are egalitarian, and US Americans, the Dutch, Australians, and the Scandinavians are more the anomalies than the norm. US American and Dutch leaders have been taught to lead and manage as facilitators. The two styles of leadership are entirely different. The point here is that in hierarchical cultures, you must begin at the top of the organization and cascade the message down and throughout for it to be taken seriously.

How do you do this? You begin by making sure that your C-suite and executive teams are fully engaged in creating cultures of belonging and inclusion. Each of these executives must have an elevator pitch about why this is important and what it means to them. They must hold meetings with their direct reports to deliver this pitch and talk about the social and financial gains to be made by engaging with this initiative, including a conversation about ESG. Then, you must ask them to cascade that message down to their direct reports and managers throughout middle management.

Simultaneously, you must introduce scalable and affordable digital competency-based-learning solutions from the **Bottom-up** to squeeze the middle.

Chapter 18

FUTURE TRENDS IN THE 21ST CENTURY

INVESTORS NOW DEMAND INFORMATION ABOUT companies' ESG initiatives before making decisions. Governments are becoming active in introducing ESG legislation at the national and regional levels, thus placing a requirement on companies to honor such practices. Social injustice has become headline news worldwide, leading inclusion—and its benefits—to become a fixture of the global business mindset. As such, the challenges, dimensions, and issues related to ESG—notably, the *S* of the equation—will become ever more significant in the 21st century. In the first chapter, we looked at three critical phenomena that highlight the ever-quickening evolution of cultural and social interaction in the 21st century. It is useful, therefore, to look at these phenomena's likely trajectories as humanity moves into the second quarter of this century.

ONGOING TRENDS

A Post-Pandemic Business World

The COVID-19 pandemic meant that businesses from Helsinki to Houston to Hyderabad began primarily operating with staff members working remotely. As we move into the 21st century, 74 percent of companies will likely retain large numbers of their once on-site workforce in remote positions. For business leaders, responding equitably across diverse and remote locations is an ongoing inclusion challenge.[18]

Thanks to the pandemic, the concept of working remotely—known as *le télétravail* in French, *el teletrabajo* in Spanish, and "remote wakeup" in Japanese—can therefore be considered the primary transformation of the 21st-century business world. Governments in Europe are already being asked to draft specific workers' rights provisions for remote employees.

This has required the large-scale remodeling of team structures—across vast distances—within international businesses worldwide. In a post-pandemic world, team composition is ever more frequently based on three critical criteria: employees working remotely full-time; employees returning to the office; and employees adopting a "hybrid" model, with part of the week spent in the office.

Managers who have never before had to think about life beyond their national environment suddenly find themselves coping with the direct responsibility of team members in other countries—and even on different continents.

This has inevitably brought inclusion to the forefront of business life, as it is essential to the long-term survival, and thriving, of such team structures.

The large numbers of remote workers in wildly diverse locations give business leaders a continued responsibility to strive to implement a social and operational ESG-based culture throughout their organizations. As we have observed, companies that are not successful at inclusion underperform in every industry sector.

In today's harsh global business environment, a lack of internal diversity can jeopardize the very existence of an organization.

Digital Nomads

As mentioned in earlier chapters, the concept of the digital nomad—individuals who work in a geographically independent Wi-Fi-enabled global location of their choice—will emerge as the other incredible metamorphosis of the 21st-century post-pandemic business world. Many employers favor this principle as it avoids overhead costs, while employees enjoy the stimulation of working in a new and exciting environment. As we enter the second quarter of this century, more people will consider adopting the digital nomad lifestyle. As such, the increase in officially remote jobs is a continuing trend.

Governments worldwide recognize the benefits of temporary work visas because remote digital workers bring money into the local economy. Some forty-four countries around the world are now offering digital nomad visas globally. It is thought that there are currently thirty-five million digital nomads of all nationalities living in different locations throughout the world. Digital nomads are evenly split by gender and are considered to represent an economic value of $787 billion (USD) annually. Studies show that if the world's digital nomads represented a single country, that country would have the forty-first-largest population of any nation on Earth. Currently, one-third of the world's digital nomads originate from the USA. Countries thought to be soon to introduce digital nomad visas (as of November 2022) include Belize, Brazil, Colombia, Indonesia, Montenegro, North Macedonia, Serbia, South Africa, Sri Lanka, and Thailand.

It is thought that 35 percent of digital nomads are employed by an international company, while 28 percent are freelancers for one or more businesses. This equates to over twenty million remote workers who would be the prime beneficiaries of a global awareness and inclusion initiative, whatever the size of the enterprise involved. This number is only going to increase in the coming years.[19]

European Union

The free movement of workers is one of the four fundamental pillars of the European Union. The free-movement pillar provides workers with the rights to individual free activity and residence, of entry and residence for family members, and to work in another EU member state. In the first decade of the 21st century, internal EU migration primarily involved the east-to-west movement of people from the new—poorer—member states to the more prosperous EU countries. This has now balanced out, as employment opportunity is more evenly spread among the EU member states.[20]

Migratory movement within the member states of the EU will therefore continue to be a significant cultural and human event in the coming decades of the 21st century. This is due both to the economic situation, as mentioned, and to the familiarity that young EU citizens now have with moving around the bloc. In the meantime, official negotiations are currently being held with Albania, Moldova, Montenegro, North Macedonia, Serbia, Turkey, and Ukraine regarding the ability of each of these countries to join the EU. Three other countries are officially on the EU waiting list to be given "candidate" status at some point soon: Bosnia and Herzegovina, Georgia, and Kosovo. This will enrich the already enormous diversity of EU citizenry and further enhance the benefit and practicality of inclusion initiatives throughout the member states.

The International Equal Pay Day Initiative

International Equal Pay Day is an initiative of the United Nations and is usually celebrated on September 18. Some countries acknowledge it on the date that symbolizes how far into the new year the average median-wage woman must work to have earned the same amount that the average male earned by the end of the previous year. The initiative is expected to gain more prominence in future years. It represents the long-standing efforts made by the UN toward achieving equal pay for work of equal value.

Women are paid less than men worldwide, with the average gender pay gap thought to be 20 percent globally. Gender equality and the empowerment of women and girls are initiatives that continue to be held back due to the persistence of historical and structural unequal power relations between women and men, poverty, and inequalities and disadvantages in access to resources and opportunities, all issues that limit women's and girls' capabilities. Progress on narrowing that gap has been slow. While equal pay for men and women has been widely endorsed, applying it in practice has been difficult.

To ensure that no one is left behind, the Sustainable Development Goals (SDGs) address the need to achieve gender equality and the empowerment of all women and girls. Furthermore, the SDGs promote by seeking full and productive employment and decent work for all women and men, including young people and persons with disabilities, and equal pay for work of equal value. Mainstreaming a gender perspective is crucial to implementing the 2030 Agenda for Sustainable Development.

Achieving equal pay is an important milestone for human rights and gender equality. It requires the effort of the entire world community, and more work remains to be done. The United Nations, including UN Women and the International Labour Organization, invites member states and civil society, women's and community-based organizations, and feminist groups, as well as businesses and workers' and employers' organizations, to promote equal pay for work of equal value and the economic empowerment of women and girls.[21]

ENHANCING BUSINESS SUCCESS IN THE 21ST CENTURY

Throughout this book, we have explained the significance of cultural competency and inclusion, which benefits companies, countries, and public bodies. For companies, the value of inclusion can be seen in bottom-line productivity and—in turn—the share-price performance of the enterprise. Inclusion initiatives can improve the productivity level of an entire nation and the performance of a publicly owned organization.

However, an inclusive workplace is not inspired by sound intentions alone, or from an outside consultant's report. There are specific steps that can be taken to ensure that the benefits of inclusion are realized. As we have observed in previous chapters of this book, at the human level, inclusion increases employee engagement and, thus, enhances idea generation. Essential steps that any organization can take to actually "make it happen" throughout the enterprise are as follows:

- Inclusion will only be successful if the desire and initiative come from the enterprise's senior leaders. If implemented solely as an HR policy item, inclusion will not reap the possible benefits for the company.

- The example and tone established by senior leadership can be fostered at all levels of the organization—both "up and down" and from peer to peer. This includes remote teams and recruitment processes.

- The ability of employees to express themselves to their direct managers is key to inclusion success. This becomes especially crucial with teams of remote employees, which may be spread across a vast geography and thus composed of diverse cultures.

- Employees can be included in the "inclusion journey" itself by being asked to share their ideas about how inclusion—and, therefore, diversity—can be enhanced and improved within the organization.

MAKING THE S OF THE ESG EQUATION MEASURABLE

As we have outlined throughout this book, business success in the coming decades of the 21st century will require a lot more cultural competency and awareness than was necessary for the decision-making processes of the past. As we have outlined in previous chapters, the "awareness" factor is all-encompassing. It includes:

- the self-awareness and cultural competency of company leaders;

- the recognition of the cultural, social, and diversity existing within an organization;

- the understanding of how a company compares to its competitors in terms of cultural and social inclusion.

As we have observed in previous chapters, the best overall framework for achieving awareness is that of the ESG (environmental, social, and governance) principle.

According to a report compiled by CNBC, most investors are focusing on the ESG dimensions of an enterprise, which—as we have already seen—can make or break business success. The *S* is the most challenging element to quantify but can be considered more critical than the other elements. A 2021 global survey by BNP Paribas covering more than three hundred companies found that 51 percent of investors thought the *S* to be the most difficult to analyze and embed in investment strategies. This is primarily because there is a wide variance in the social metrics of every enterprise. However, the basic premise of the *S* is the sense of belonging of *all* members of the enterprise, which may extend to any supplier network involved. For analysts, the measurable parts of the *S* part of the ESG equation pertain to financial inclusion, income equality, and minority equality.[22]

S&P describes the absence of these measurables as social factors that may risk a company's financial performance. In doing so, S&P outlines two major *S*-related issues that may impact business operations:

- How can a company's workforce requirements present future composition problems for the organization?

- What future demographic changes could shrink the market for a company's products or services?

ESG information is vital in measuring how a company's actions impact people's lives. This statement ultimately includes the lives of the employees, the supply chain, and the customers of a given enterprise. This is why governments seek to introduce inclusion legislation. Such legislation encourages outside investment in the nation's companies and promotes growth and stability.

Measuring the *S* factor has therefore become critical. The obstacles to doing so can be considered the challenge of quantification, erratic reporting, and the lack of standardization of inclusion, diversity, equity, and belonging. These challenges can be compounded when multiple and diverse overseas locations are added to the analysis of a would-be investor. The *S* does, therefore, need to be measurable, both for internal (C-suite) and external (investor) use. Companies should start reporting consistent *S* data, and investors should specifically ask for it. In turn and in time, agencies measuring ESG data should align with each other to aid in standardization.

As already stated, every organization is different. However, a source that can be useful in reaching some standardization in measuring the *S* is the United Nations. The UN's SDGs provide a framework that can measure social impact via more than 160 associated targets (such as gender equality) that can be applied as and when they may be relevant to an enterprise. As also highlighted previously, this is where governments can lend measurability to the equation by legislating for specific minority quotas and gender equality in companies.

ESG AND ITS IMPACT ON COMPANY PERFORMANCE

In a broader context, the measurement and visibility of ESG in an enterprise are becoming imperative for business success in the 21st century. According to PricewaterhouseCoopers (PwC):

- 83 percent of consumers want companies to shape ESG best practices;

- 91 percent of business leaders think they are responsible for acting on ESG issues;

- 86 percent of employees want to work for a company that supports the same issues that they do.

The PwC study also showed that consumers aged seventeen to thirty-eight are twice as likely as older consumers to consider ESG issues when purchasing. This straightforward sentence entirely explains the connection between ESG and company performance and, therefore, the value companies need to apply to the ESG equation moving forward.[23]

The Sustainability Accounting Standards Board (SASB) is a nonprofit, US-based organization dedicated to reporting the impact of ESG factors on the financial performance of companies. The SASB further classified the three pillars of the ESG equation into eleven measurables of ESG performance. The ultimate goal is to provide an ESG score that can be used both internally by an organization and externally by analysts as a measurement tool.

An ESG score is based on how an organization is seen to be relating to ESG issues, including any goals it may have set for itself. However, plans not published by the enterprise in the public domain will not impact the enterprise's ESG score. Industry benchmarks are a valuable component in ESG valuation, as they can best measure how a company's performance compares with its competitors.

ESG ratings impact profitability, regardless of what industry your company is in. People like to know that the companies they interact with and buy from are companies that do good in the world.

Examples of the correlation between ESG actions and profitability include the following:

- Bayer is based in Germany and is one of the world's largest pharmaceutical companies. The enterprise consistently receives a good rating regarding the management of its relevant ESG issues. Company profits have risen by an average of 22.2 percent over the past three years.[24]

- Eni is an Italian energy company with global operations. It is rated as "gold class" in terms of how it combines its ESG narrative with actual execution. The company has seen its net profit margin improve by 13.45 percent over the past two years.[25]

- Linde is a multinational chemical enterprise that has consistently followed its ESG initiatives, and, in 2021, it was recognized as "Best-in-Class for Sustainability Disclosure Practices." Since then, the company has seen an average annual profit increase of 9 percent.[26]

- Microsoft is a United States–based enterprise that produces consumer electronics, computer software, and personal computers. In 2019, the company received the maximum recognition for its ESG practices. Since then, its profits have increased by an average of 17.8 percent per year.[27]

- Texas Instruments is a United States–based technology enterprise and one of the ten largest semiconductor companies worldwide. It regularly ranks in the top ten companies in the United States for ESG rating. The company has seen its profits increase by an average of 18.3 percent since 2019.[28]

CONCLUDING THOUGHTS

In this book, we have highlighted several successful and innovative cultural and inclusion initiatives in the corporate, academic, and government sectors. Regardless of the entity, the intent to make inclusion a priority must come from and be championed by the top. Very large organizations tend to employ a chief talent officer, chief diversity officer, or a chief people officer to monitor the pace and progress of any inclusion initiative. However, regardless of the size of the organization, most don't have the budget for a team of people to run those programs. Additionally, in 2023, we are already seeing that companies are drastically cutting those budgets. That said, organizations should look for digital cultural intelligence learning solutions that are scalable and easily socialized throughout the enterprise. These solutions can drive inclusion and cultural competency with or without a team of people to run them. One such solution is GoWorldWise. com, which covers two hundred countries in over fifty languages and includes a diagnostic report that ties organizational learning directly back to measuring the *S* in ESG. An added bonus is all of the leadership features they include are designed to develop the cultural competencies needed to grow business performance including sales and operations.

We know that in every culture, people communicate differently, build relationships differently, develop trust differently, show respect differently, and even think of time differently. With heightened cultural intelligence and a particular cultural competency, you can transform any organization into an inclusive one, where everyone feels seen, heard, and respected, while simultaneously driving revenue, share price, and ESG that will attract the employees and investors of today and far into the 21st century.

Endnotes

1. Johnson, Whitney, Dawn Klinghoffer et al., and Melissa Daimler. "The Value of Belonging at Work." Harvard Business Review, December 21, 2021. https://hbr.org/2019/12/the-value-of-belonging-at-work.

2. "Free Movement of Workers: Fact Sheets on the European Union: European Parliament." Fact Sheets on the European Union | European Parliament. Accessed April 26, 2023. https://www.europarl.europa.eu/factsheets/en/sheet/41/free-movement-of-workers.

3. Johnson, Klinghoffer, and Daimler. "The Value of Belonging at Work."

4. "Hauptnavigation." zur Startseite der Bundesagentur für Arbeit. Aoife Kennedy, 2022. https://www.arbeitsagentur.de/en/employment-law.

5. "Workforce Development for Adults 50+." The Center for Workforce Inclusion, November 29, 2021. https://www.centerforworkforceinclusion.org/.

6. "Hauptnavigation."

7. "Inclusion and Diversity at Accenture." Accenture. Accessed April 26, 2023. https://www.accenture.com/us-en/about/inclusion-diversity-index.

8. "Diageo Ranks Number Two Globally in EQUILEAP's 2023 Gender Equality Global Report." www.diageo.com. Accessed April 26, 2023. https://www.diageo.com/en/news-and-media/stories/2023/diageo-ranks-number-two-globally-in-equileap-s-2023-gender-equality-global-report.

9. "Equality and Belonging Groups." Gap Inc. Accessed April 26, 2023. https://www.gapinc.com/en-us/values/equality-belonging/equality-and-belonging-groups

10. Medtronic. "Diversity Networks & Ergs." Medtronic. Accessed April 26, 2023. https://www.medtronic.com/us-en/our-impact/diversity-networks-ergs.html.

11. Dixon-Fyle, Sundiatu, Kevin Dolan, Dame Vivian Hunt, and Sara Prince. "Diversity Wins: How Inclusion Matters." McKinsey & Company. McKinsey & Company, May 19, 2020. https://www.mckinsey.com/featured-insights/diversity-andinclusion/diversity-wins-how-inclusion-matters.

12. Branch, S., & Sethi, B. (2016). (working paper). *Building Cross-Cultural Competence in an Increasingly Global Workforce.*

13. "Unemployed Persons." Statistics Denmark. Accessed April 26, 2023. https://www.dst.dk/en/Statistik/emner/arbejde-og-indkomst/arbejdsloese.

14. "Gender." Maersk. Accessed April 26, 2023. https://www.maersk.com/careers/ diversity-equity-and-inclusion/gender#:~:text=A%20key%20gender%20 equity%20target%20for%202025%20is,level%2C%20driven%20by%20 affinity%20groups%2C%20programmes%20and%20initiatives.

15. "Sodexo #1 French Company for Gender Balance in Top Management." Sodexo India. Accessed April 26, 2023. https://in.sodexo.com/medias/sodexo-1-french-companyfor-ge-1.html.

16. "Well over One in Four People in Germany Had a Migrant Background in 2021." Federal Statistical Office, April 19, 2022 https://www.destatis.de/EN/ Press/2022/04/PE22_162_125.html.

17. "Home - CSO - Central Statistics Office." CSO, August 28, 2019. https://www.cso.ie/en/index.html.

18. "How COVID-19 Has Pushed Companies over the Technology Tipping Point-and Transformed Business Forever." McKinsey & Company. McKinsey & Company, October 5, 2020. https://www.mckinsey.com/capabilities/strategy-and-corporate-finance/our-insights/how-covid-19-has-pushed-companies-over-the-technology-tippingpoint-and-transformed-business-forever.

19. This text provides general information. Statista assumes no liability for the information given being complete or correct. Due to varying update cycles, statistics can display more up-to-date data than referenced in the text. "Topic: Digital Nomads."Statista. Accessed April 26, 2023. https://www.statista.com/ topics/9259/digital-nomads/.

20. "About." Migration Mobilities Bristol. Accessed April 26, 2023. https://migration.bristol.ac.uk/.

21. "Gender Equality and Women's Empowerment." United Nations. United Nations.Accessed April 26, 2023. https://www.un.org/sustainabledevelopment/ gender-equality/.

22. Stevens, Pippa. "ESG Index Funds Hit $250 Billion as Pandemic Accelerates Impact Investing Boom." CNBC. CNBC, September 2, 2020. https://www.

cnbc.com/2020/09/02/esg-index-funds-hit-250-billion-as-us-investor-rolein-boom-grows.html.

23. PricewaterhouseCoopers. "How Much Does the Public Care about ESG?" PwC. Accessed April 26, 2023. https://www.pwc.com/gx/en/services/sustainability/publications/cop26/how-much-doesthe-public-care-about-esg-pwc-cop26.html.

24. "Risk Rating Company Report - Bayer." Accessed April 26, 2023. https://www.bayer.com/sites/default/files/Sustainalytics_RiskRatingsSummaryReport_Byer%20AG_April%202021.pdf.

25. "Key Operating and Financial Results - Eni." Accessed April 26, 2023. https://www.eni.com/assets/documents/press-release/migrated/2022-en/02/eni-fourthquarter-2021-ceo-claudio-descalzi-comments-results.pdf.

26. "Reporting Center." Praxair, Inc. and Linde AG have merged to create Linde plc-a global leader of engineering and industrial, process and specialty gases with product and service offerings in over 100 countries. Accessed April 26, 2023. https://www.linde.com/sustainable-development/reporting-center.

27. "Recognition: Microsoft CSR." Microsoft. Accessed April 26, 2023. https://www.microsoft.com/en-us/corporate-responsibility/recognition.

28. "Board Oversight of ESG Matters." esg. Accessed April 26, 2023. https://www.ti.com/about-ti/citizenship-community/overview/ESG.html.

Contributor Bios

CHRIS RICHARDSON

Chris Richardson has lived in seven countries on three continents, performing both global and regional roles in the areas of mobility and talent management. A native of the United Kingdom, his career has taken him to cities such as Geneva, New York, Paris, and Zürich. As managing editor of World Trade Resource, Chris is responsible for the content integrity of publications shared with two hundred countries around the world. He now resides in Athens, Greece. Chris speaks French and German in addition to his mother tongue, English. Chris is an avid traveler who enjoys returning to the countries in which he has lived and exploring new ones. Chris is a graduate of the University of the West of England and the Universität Kassel in Germany.

CHRISTINE SPERR

Christine Sperr has thirty years of experience in global talent management and mobility, spanning the United States, Asia, Europe, and the Middle East. Early in her career, she focused on large-scale projects for clients by structuring their expatriate services' support delivery. Her clients included Procter & Gamble's operations in Asia and the market entry of General Motors into Thailand. Excelling as a general manager, Christine has assumed leadership roles for direct service delivery operations in each region in which she has worked, lived, and thrived. At the same time, Christine is an intrepid traveler and immensely enjoys the genuine experience of learning about diverse cultures and people. Outside of her professional relocation activities, her passion is to lead small groups in traveling to less frequented and challenging countries (such as Afghanistan, Iran, Iraq, and Yemen). A graduate of the University of Colorado in the United States, Christine is currently based in Dubai, where she serves as managing director for Santa Fe Relocation.

ERIKA GONZALEZ MERCEDES

Erika Gonzalez Mercedes is a passionate leader who has dedicated her career to making workplaces more equitable and inclusive. She currently serves as the diversity business partner at one of the most well-known tech companies on the planet. Prior to attaining this position, she served as the head of diversity and inclusion at Audible, where she was responsible for leading the creation and implementation of the organization's global diversity, equity, and inclusion strategy, program development, and deployment. She worked closely with senior management to develop, deliver, and promote innovative practices, establish metrics and benchmarks, and create the road map that supports Audible's ability to empower, engage, and unlock the potential of global talent.

Erika has a diverse background in the fields of marketing, procurement, and e-commerce. Before joining Audible, she spent seven years at Wyndham Worldwide serving in various positions across business units and leading diversity and inclusion initiatives. Formerly, Erika held roles as an analyst and manager at Wakefern Food Corporation and Liberty Mutual Group. She is an active participant in nonprofit organizations. She has served as a board member for the Prospanica (the national society of Hispanic MBAs) New Jersey chapter, as the Morris County Diversity and Inclusion Committee chair for the Society for Human Resource Management, and as a volunteer for the Big Brothers Big Sisters of America program, and she contributes as a mentor for young professionals in her community.

Erika is a graduate of the College of New Jersey, where she received a bachelor of science in business administration marketing, and later obtained an MBA in health-care administration from Seton Hall University. She also completed the Executive Education for Sustainability Leadership program at Harvard T.H. Chan School of Public Health. Erika currently resides in New Jersey with her husband, Enmanuel, and their three sons.

GIANCARLO FRANCESE

Giancarlo Francese serves as the senior program officer for the Bill & Melinda Gates Foundation managing several global health programs. Giancarlo identifies new opportunities and innovative management approaches in providing equitable health-care solutions in low- and middle-income countries.

Giancarlo has more than twenty years of experience in the pharmaceutical industry R&D and has held senior positions with such companies as Novartis and Teva Pharmaceutical Industries. His scope of work has included drug development in the early-, late-, launch-, and post-marketing stages. His focus and expertise are in global health programs in partnership with external global health key players. He has worked in collaboration with external organizations for the development and introduction of new tropical medicines with a special focus on the innovative treatment of malaria for adult and pediatric populations. Giancarlo pioneered and implemented innovative R&D approaches for cost-saving and patient-centric care and, thus, the expansion of drug accessibility to a wider population.

Giancarlo holds a Master of Science (MSc) in chemistry from the University of Pavia in Italy and a PhD in supramolecular chemistry from the University of Bern in Switzerland. He resides in Seattle, Washington.

GUILLERMO GONZALEZ-PRIETO

Guillermo Gonzalez-Prieto is a native of Madrid and a global talent and mobility professional. He currently serves as mobility lead for Cargill in Spain. After graduating from the Universidad Complutense de Madrid, he began his career with Alcatel. Subsequent promotions have taken him from Madrid to Paris and then to Doha, in senior roles with Nokia, Baker Hughes, and Qatar Petroleum (now QatarEnergy). He considers his cultural transitions to have been a positive life experience that made him more empathetic and truly helped him create a global mindset. Guillermo graduated from professional coaching programs in Paris and Qatar. Guillermo has recently returned to Spain and is based in Barcelona.

HELEN NEWMAN

Helen Newman has been in the international education space for over twenty years and in higher education for more than a decade. Helen is New York University's associate director of Immigration and Mobility Services at the Office of Global Services (OGS). At OGS, Helen leads the Outbound Team, which assists thousands of domestic and international students with their mobility needs for studying abroad. Helen also provides complex immigration advising for NYU researchers and faculty members. Additionally, she delivers global-mobility support to NYU's international assignment population and is a US Designated School Official. She has also served in leadership roles in her professional association via NAFSA's Education Abroad Knowledge Community.

Prior to landing at NYU, Helen cotaught international undergrads in addition to developing high-profile internships and cultivating partnerships with the United Nations, international NGOs, global nonprofits, and Fortune 500 companies. She has also managed a J-1 high school exchange program and regularly volunteers for humanitarian causes. Helen holds a master of arts from NYU in international education and a bachelor of arts from Elizabethtown College in political science.

ISMAEL KOSSIH

Ismael Kossih is a native of Brussels, Belgium. He has worked with global companies such as Chanel, Chopard, and Gucci, and his career has taken him from Brussels to London to Dubai. These locations and experiences have helped him develop a global mindset that has proved invaluable as he builds sales and marketing strategies and identifies opportunities in extremely competitive global markets, attaining leverage that he wouldn't otherwise have.

JIM FRAWLEY

Jim Frawley is an accomplished author, a Columbia University–certified executive coach, and the host of the *Bellwether Hub with*

Jim Frawley podcast. His twenty-year corporate career encompasses such positions as C-suite, chief of staff, business management, and executive communications with global companies such as BNY Mellon, TD Bank, and UBS. Jim has collaborated on product launches on the New York Stock Exchange and has created and implemented international corporate training programs along with complex marketing and PR strategies. Jim's coaching and training activities have taken him to eight countries, where he has worked with such enterprises as Cedars-Sinai Medical Center, Lincoln Financial, Morgan Stanley, *TIME*, and Verizon.

SABRINA KENT

As executive vice president at the National LGBT Chamber of Commerce (NGLCC), Sabrina Kent serves as a member of NGLCC's executive leadership and supports the efforts of its board of directors in advocating for the economic empowerment of LGBT-owned businesses both within the US and globally. Sabrina's work focuses on strategic projects across the organization. Sabrina oversees NGLCC's Supplier Diversity Initiative and is also a member of the NGLCC Global team, focusing on the division's growing work in other countries. Sabrina has a Bachelor of Arts in Philosophy and Sexuality from Rollins College.

Sabrina was named the 2014 Sojourner Truth Awardee for Combined Academic and Activist Work by the Rollins College Sexuality, Women's & Gender Studies Executive Committee, and she served as editor-in-chief of the *Independent* magazine, a 2015 Columbia Press Association Gold Crown Award recipient.

In January 2019, Sabrina was recognized by *Business Equality Magazine* as a Top 40 LGBT Leader Under 40 and was named to the board of directors of Q Street, an organization focused on supporting LGBT advocates and lobbyists in Washington, DC. In June 2020, Sabrina was named to the inaugural *Crain's New York Business* list of Notable LGBTQ Leaders and Executives. In June of 2022, Sabrina was named to the inaugural Colorado LGBTQ Chamber of Commerce Under 40 Business Leaders.

About the Author

STEPHAN M. BRANCH HAS LED both privately held and multi-billion-dollar publicly traded companies in the US, Asia, Latin America, and Europe. During his tenure at those companies, he was responsible for a total of fifty-five countries and lived on five continents. He has been instrumental in global IPOs while simultaneously creating explosive growth to meet the very high expectations of investors and boards.

He has a Master's degree from George Washington University and is a graduate of Harvard Law School's International Negotiation Program. He is multi-lingual and has served multiple terms on the Board of Directors of the National Foreign Trade Council and is the Founder and CEO of World Trade Resource (WTR) headquartered in New York City. Under his guidance, WTR was named as a Top 10 Global Leadership Development Firm for 2023.

Branch was recently named as one of the 10 Must-Watch Innovators to follow in 2023. The secret to his success is that he fully grasps how leadership, cultural intelligence, and inclusion coalesce to create extraordinary leaders with a transformative impact on revenue, business valuation, and ESG.